Voyageurs, Lumberjacks, and Farmers

In her painting Shooting the Rapids, *artist Frances Anne Hopkins (1838-1919) re-created the daring journeys made by the voyageurs through the Upper Great Lakes region.*

Voyageurs, Lumberjacks, and Farmers

Pioneers of the Midwest

Kieran Doherty

The Oliver Press, Inc.
Minneapolis

The Oliver Press, Inc.
Charlotte Square
5707 West 36th Street
Minneapolis, MN 55416-2510

Library of Congress Cataloging-in-Publication Data
Doherty, Kieran.
Voyageurs, lumberjacks, and farmers : pioneers of the midwest / Kieran Doherty.
    p.   cm. — (Shaping America ; v. 5)
    Summary: Discusses lives of eight people who played a significant role in the exploration of territory and founding of settlements in the American Midwest. Includes Antoine Cadillac, Charles Langlade, Jean de Sable, George Rogers Clark, Rufus Putnam, Julien Dubuque, and Josiah and Abigail Snelling.

ISBN 1-881508-54-4 (lib. bdg.)

1. Pioneers—Middle West—Biography—Juvenile literature. 2. Frontier and pioneer life—Middle West—Juvenile literature. 3. Middle West—Biography—Juvenile literature. 4. Middle West—History—Juvenile literature. [1. Pioneers. 2. Explorers. 3. Frontier and pioneer life—Middle West. 4. Middle West—History.] I. Title. II. Series.

F350.5 .D64 2004
977'.01'0922—dc21
[B]   2002041035

ISBN 1-881508-54-4
Printed in the United States of America
10 09 08 07 06 05 04   8 7 6 5 4 3 2 1

Contents

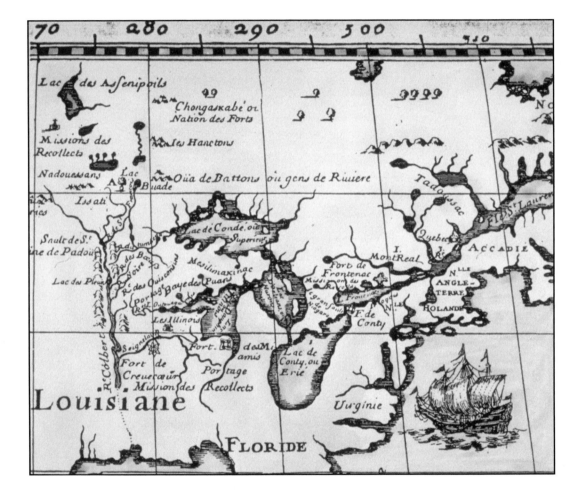

Introduction

For thousands of years before the first European set foot in the region we know today as the midwestern United States, the vast fertile land that includes Michigan, Ohio, Indiana, Illinois, Wisconsin, Minnesota, Iowa, and North and South Dakota was home to a diverse mix of people. These Native Americans were the descendants of immigrants who came to North America from Asia by way of the Bering Strait land bridge, probably in search of game. The land bridge formed during one of the ice ages, when glaciers spread south across Canada into New England and many portions of the Midwest. Enough of the planet's water was frozen to lower the ocean levels and enlarge shorelines. The 56-mile-wide Bering Strait could have then become passable on foot.

Alaska was not covered by ice due to low rainfalls and snowfalls, so the Asians probably lived there until temporary melts made it possible for them to migrate south. As long ago as 20,000 B.C., some of these Asian hunters made their way into the central sections of the United States and Canada. Over the

This map of eastern North America was drawn by Louis Hennepin (1640-1701?), a Franciscan priest and explorer who came to Canada in 1675.

next several thousand years, groups of people moved farther east to the heavily forested, game-rich lands that stretched from Minnesota to the Atlantic Ocean. For many generations, these Native Americans had no idea of a world other than their own. This began to change in 1492, when Christopher Columbus arrived in the New World.

In the years just after Columbus's first voyage, the exploration of North America began in earnest. The first explorers were Spanish adventurers and soldiers who swept north and west from the Caribbean and Mexico to explore large parts of the

The voyage of Christopher Columbus (1451-1506) sparked great interest in the exploration and settlement of North America.

Americas. While the Spanish were establishing colonies and trading centers throughout South and Central America and the Caribbean, the French were opening another frontier, far to the north, first in Canada and then in the region around the Great Lakes and the Mississippi River.

Unlike the Dutch and British who came later and built such settlements as New Amsterdam (New York) and Boston and Plymouth in Massachusetts, these early French explorers were not primarily interested in building settlements in the New World. Instead, their goals were to establish a profitable trade with the Indians and to claim rich territory for France. Many French explorers also hoped to find the Northwest Passage, the fabled water route that would have enabled traders to sail directly from the Atlantic Ocean to the Pacific Ocean, and then on to the riches of China and India. The efforts to discover a route through or around North America began with the voyages of John Cabot in the 1490s. He was unsuccessful, of course, as no such sea route exists. But the efforts made by the explorers opened much of the region to traders and, eventually, to settlers.

In May 1535, Jacques Cartier, looking for the Northwest Passage, discovered instead the mouth of the St. Lawrence River. He made his way along the river to a mountain he called Mont Real (Mount Royal), and visited the Huron village of Hochelaga located there. This village eventually grew to be the modern city of Montreal.

Jacques Cartier (1491-1557) and his first meeting with the Hurons at Hochelaga in 1535

It was many years before any lasting French settlements were established in the region explored and claimed for France by Cartier. Only a few scattered attempts were made to even explore the area until the years between 1603 and 1616, when Samuel de Champlain sailed beyond Montreal to explore a lake in the mountains between upstate New York and Vermont that he named Lake Champlain. He gave the European world its first knowledge of the Great Lakes after canoeing along sections of the coasts of Lakes Huron and Ontario.

The next great steps in exploration were taken by Pierre Esprit Radisson (1632-1710) and his brother-in-law Médard Chouart, sieur des Groseilliers, in 1659. They left the settlement of Trois-Rivières (Three Rivers) and made their way to the far western end of Lake Superior. From there they journeyed inland to Sioux and Ojibwa villages in what is now Minnesota, becoming the first Europeans to travel so far. The brothers-in-law returned to Trois-Rivières laden with furs.

In 1671, Pierre Esprit Radisson accepted a gift of food while Médard Chouart, sieur des Groseilliers, greeted a Native American chief at Charles Fort in Quebec. Groseilliers helped to build this trading post.

An unlikely pair, Louis Joliet (1645-1700), a fur trader, and Jacques Marquette (1637-1675), a Jesuit priest, became in 1673 the first Europeans to explore the upper Mississippi River. They paddled first on the Fox River and then on the Wisconsin to reach the Mississippi. They then traveled downriver to where the Ohio River meets the Mississippi before returning north.

By the middle of the seventeenth century, the French had established something like peaceful relations with the Native Americans of the lands around

The exploration route of Jacques Marquette and Louis Joliet

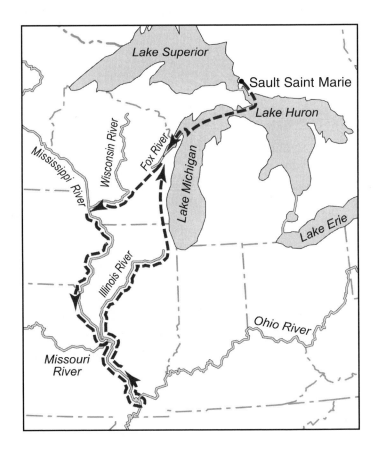

the Great Lakes. These friendly ties were built on commerce. The French provided the native people with trade goods, including weapons and liquor, in exchange for valuable furs. Realizing the need for more permanent trading headquarters, a few voyageurs began establishing small settlements on the frontier.

This book includes the stories of two of these brave trapper-explorers. The first, Antoine Laumet de Lamothe Cadillac, established a trading post and fort that became the city of Detroit, Michigan. The second, Jean du Sable, built a house and established a trading post on the banks of Lake Michigan. That tiny outpost on the frontier later grew to be the great city of Chicago, Illinois.

For many years, even as the region along the Atlantic coast became civilized and populated by the British, the land to the west of the settled regions was still wild, largely uncharted territory. In those years, much of the region was the scene of almost constant warfare. On one side were the French, with their New World capital in Canada. On the other side were the British, who wanted to move west from their established cities along the Atlantic coast. At stake was a vast territory rich in arable land, furs, and natural resources.

It was not until the end of the French and Indian Wars in 1763—when France turned control of its territory around the Great Lakes over to the British—that this region opened for settlement. Even then, however, the pace of settlement was slow. Just a few brave frontiersmen were willing to take their

A voyageur was a woodsman, boatman, or guide employed by a fur company to transport goods and supplies between remote posts throughout Canada and the Great Lakes region.

families from the relative safety of the populated settlements into the dangers of the unknown frontier.

Included in this book is the story of one such settler, Charles de Langlade, half French, half Native American, who allied himself with the British before the end of the French and Indian War and who earned fame as the first permanent settler in what is now the city of Green Bay, Wisconsin.

Langlade took up residence in Green Bay in 1765, but the real settlement of the region we know as the midwestern United States began in the years following the Revolutionary War, after Great Britain gave up claims to this huge block of land. George Rogers Clark, a frontiersman and soldier, led an expedition against a British fort located at Vincennes, Indiana, that aided the Americans during the Revolutionary War. He and some of his men stayed on, helping to settle Indiana. Another Revolutionary War hero, Rufus Putnam, was instrumental in convincing the new U.S. government to grant land to war veterans. He then led a group that founded the first settlement in Ohio.

Julien Dubuque took advantage of rapid expansion in this period to mine and trade on the banks of the Mississippi River, where the city of Dubuque, Iowa, exists today. Josiah Snelling, an accomplished soldier, built a frontier fort in Minnesota to protect the settlers coming to this new territory. The modern Twin Cities of St. Paul and Minneapolis, one of the Midwest's largest metropolitan areas, ultimately grew around this fort.

George Rogers Clark led the decisive battle to take the fort at Vincennes, Indiana, in 1779.

Some of the pioneers whose stories are included in this book explored or established tiny outposts on the frontier in hopes of obtaining riches or fame. Others were in search of new lives for themselves or their families. A few of these men were not always honorable and sometimes took advantage of the Native Americans they met. All, however, were brave people who made their mark in what was an untamed land. They all serve as out-standing examples of the courageous pioneer spirit that made, and continues to make, the United States a great nation.

Chapter One

Antoine Cadillac
and
Detroit, Michigan

O n a summer day in 1701, a fleet of canoes made its way up the narrow river that joins Lakes St. Clair and Erie. The canoes were filled with armed soldiers, settlers, and Indians. They had traveled south down the length of the river the previous day, camping overnight on an island. Now they slowly moved back north, alongside tree-lined bluffs. In one of the canoes rode Antoine Laumet de Lamothe Cadillac, a French adventurer and soldier. He was searching the entire length of the river for the best landing place, a place where he could build a fort and settlement. As he searched, Cadillac spied a small hill on the river's north bank. It was the perfect location for a settlement. He signaled for the canoes to pull to shore.

Antoine Laumet de Lamothe Cadillac (1658-1730) lands at the site of Detroit, Michigan, in 1701.

Within days, a palisade, or barrier, of oak pilings was constructed. Homes, warehouses, and a church were built within this wall. The little settlement was named Ville de Troit, or Village of the Straits. Over time, the "ville" was dropped and the town grew into the great city we know as Detroit.

Cadillac was born on March 5, 1658, in a brick house on a cobblestone street bordering the public square in the town of St. Nicolas-de-la-Grave, France. His father, Jean Laumet, was a lawyer and judge. Jeanne de Péchagut, his mother, was the daughter of a local landowner. Married in 1646, his parents had at least eight children.

Little is known about Cadillac's childhood in the village about 30 miles from the city of Toulouse. Records show he was baptized as Antoine Laumet five days after his birth. Historians think, based on the quality of his writing as a man, that he was well educated as a boy. He was probably a student at an academy in Toulouse where one of the professors was a friend of his father.

According to a memoir written by Cadillac, he joined the army in about 1677, following the death of his parents. Exactly where he served and what rank he reached is not clear, since he claimed different backgrounds at different times in his life.

By 1683, Antoine Cadillac had reached New France (France's North American colonial empire, now Canada), landing in Port Royal in what was then known as Acadia. (Port Royal today is the city of Annapolis Royal, Nova Scotia.) At the time, the French and British were waging an as-yet-

The original name of the Canadian province of Nova Scotia was Acadia, first used in 1603. Acadia later referred to all the territory between the St. Lawrence River and the Gulf of the St. Lawrence and Atlantic Ocean, including New Brunswick and eastern Maine.

The French garrison at Port Royal, Nova Scotia

undeclared war in the New World. The British had, for the most part, settled along the eastern seaboard between the Allegheny Mountains and the Atlantic Ocean. The French were in control of Acadia, the St. Lawrence River, and the towns of Quebec and Montreal, as well as the territory around the Great Lakes and along the Mississippi River as far south as New Orleans.

Soon after his arrival in the French colonies, Cadillac began trading with the local Indians. He joined the crew of Captain François Guyon, a shipper and perhaps a privateer. As a member of Guyon's crew, Cadillac studied and became familiar with the conditions of the Atlantic seaboard.

A privateer commanded a privately owned ship that was authorized by the government to attack and capture enemy ships.

The governor of the territory, Louis Alexandre de Friches, Chevalier de Ménneval, wrote that "this Cadillac, the most malicious person in the world, is a wild man driven from France for who knows what crimes." Rumors surrounded Cadillac during virtually his entire life, probably because it became known that he had changed his name.

On June 25, 1687, Cadillac married 17-year-old Marie-Thérèse Guyon, the niece of François. In the marriage contract, he called himself "Antoine de Lamothe, Esquire, Sieur de Cadillac . . . son of Mr. Jean de la Mothe, Sieur of the place called Cadillac. . . . " This was a lie. His father's sur-name—like his—was Laumet and he was a judge, not the "sieur" (lord) of Cadillac.

The assumption of this new name—with its air of nobility—may have been Cadillac's attempt to conceal some past crime. More likely, the taking of an alias was merely a means for Cadillac to get ahead in the New World. It was not unusual, in those days, for people wishing to appear noble to appropriate or invent titles.

About the time Cadillac took his new name, he tried to join the legal profession but was opposed by Louis Ménneval, the governor of Acadia. Ménneval, perhaps knowing of Cadillac's name change, neither liked nor trusted the self-made nobleman.

Soon, however, Cadillac's fortunes changed for the better. In late 1689, he was dispatched on a ship to study the coastline of Acadia. A raging storm forced the vessel far out to sea. Eventually, the ship landed in France. There, Cadillac was able to make his report in person to French authorities.

"This Cadillac . . . is an adventurer who has explored northern America and done so with application and brought back reasonably exact information," an unidentified government clerk wrote after Cadillac made his report. "It should be pointed out that if at some later time we wish to undertake some action against New York or New England, he will be a necessary actor because of his detailed knowledge of the coasts and ports."

As a reward for his services, Cadillac was made an officer of the army in Canada. He also gained the support of important figures in government, including Louis de Buade, comte de Frontenac (1620-1698), the governor of New France.

The next several years were busy ones for the newly respectable adventurer. In 1691, he helped officials in Quebec draw up plans to attack the English colony at New York. Early the next year, he was called to France, where he conferred with officials in the Ministry of Marine. He received orders to sail along the waters of the eastern coast again, making needed corrections to maps and charts used by the French.

In late 1692, Cadillac returned to Paris, armed with maps of Boston and Manhattan along with charts of the American coastline from Acadia to Virginia. King Louis XIV, in a letter to Governor Frontenac, praised Cadillac's work. With both the king and governor favorably impressed by his service, Cadillac was soon rewarded. Upon his return to Quebec in mid-1693, he was given command of Fort de Buade at Michilimackinac, a village at the narrowest point of the Straits of Mackinaw connecting Lakes Huron and Michigan.

As soon as Cadillac took command of his new post, he began exploring the lands around the Great Lakes. His goal, he wrote in a letter to one of the

While Ménneval neither liked nor trusted Cadillac, the adventurer made a good impression on Frontenac. In appointing Cadillac to his command, Frontenac described him as a man "of distinction, of great capacity and worth."

In his report to French authorities following his journey along the Atlantic seaboard, Cadillac described Boston as follows: "Two-thirds of the city is built of wood and the rest in brick or stone; the houses are pleasant and very neat; it is inhabited by merchants and sailors. There are very few gentlemen." The residents, he added, "are republican in their souls and are the sworn enemies of tyranny."

Michigan before Cadillac

Some 12,000 years before the first French explorer set foot in Michigan, the region was inhabited by a nomadic people we call Paleo-Indians. These early natives appeared in the region during the last Ice Age. As the Ice Age ended and large game vanished, a new culture developed, now known as the Archaic. These people were hunter-gatherers who lived on deer, nuts, and wild grains. By about 3000 B.C., these early residents of Michigan had learned to mine copper (found on Isle Royale and the southern shore of Lake Superior) and create tools and ornaments from the metal.

The Native Americans who met the first Europeans in the 1600s were direct descendants of these people. About 15,000 lived in Michigan in the early 1600s. Most of the Native Americans in the Great Lakes region were members of one of three Algonquian-speaking groups, the Ojibwa, Ottawa, or Potawatomi. The Wyandot, an Iroquoian-speaking group, settled near what is now Detroit.

Étienne Brûlé, a French explorer searching for a waterway to the Pacific Ocean, was probably the first European to reach Michigan, in about 1618. He was followed by other French missionaries, traders, and explorers, as fur traders from Canada extended their influence over the Great Lakes region. In 1668, Jacques Marquette, a French priest, created a mission at Sault Saint Marie in the Upper Peninsula.

Native Americans race their canoes near Sault Saint Marie in this painting by George Catlin.

officials in the Ministry of Marine, was to provide the French with "a chart with so clear an explanation that henceforth you will speak as shrewdly about it as if you had been to those places."

While Cadillac explored the lakes and commanded the fort and the 200 or so men who served there, he also earned a small fortune by trading brandy with the Indians in exchange for beaver pelts. His activities at Fort de Buade put him at odds with a group of Jesuit missionaries. The priests publicly accused Cadillac of violating a royal proclamation that outlawed trading alcohol for furs.

The headstrong, profit-minded Cadillac and the powerful Jesuits were in conflict until 1697. In that year, the depressed state of the beaver trade led Louis XIV to curtail beaver pelt trading and to close many forts in New France, including Fort de Buade. The closing of the fort brought an end to Cadillac's trading activities, at least for a time. He returned to Quebec, however, filled with plans for a grand new undertaking.

As commander at de Buade, Cadillac had explored the region around the Great Lakes. He had seen the river known as de Troit (later called the Detroit River) that connected Lakes Huron and Erie. He recognized the region's strategic and commercial importance; the Detroit River made it possible to travel from one end of the Great Lakes to the other. He desired to establish a French commercial center there to rival New York.

In 1698, Cadillac sailed to France, where he proposed founding a permanent settlement on the

Detroit River. He also proposed gathering the Indians scattered to the north near Lakes Huron and Superior at the settlement to make them permanent allies of the French. Such an arrangement, he argued, would offer protection to French interests from both the British and from unfriendly natives. The Indians, he reasoned, would bring in furs and, over time, become converted to French religion and customs.

Cadillac wanted to establish a genuine colony, not just another fort. The settlers would support themselves. The argument that the settlement would not be a drain on the French treasury surely carried much weight, for these were the years when King Louis XIV, the Sun King, was living—and spending—lavishly at the Court of Versailles.

Louis XIV (1638-1715), known as the "Sun King" because of his lavish lifestyle, fought a series of costly and deadly wars as he tried to become the ruler of all Europe.

Antoine Cadillac's plan was backed by Jérôme Phélypeaux, comte de Pontchartrain, the Minister of Marine. Early in 1700, Pontchartrain sent a message to Cadillac saying his proposal had received the king's approval. Cadillac was given money to build a fort, a grant of about 225 acres of land, and a small allowance for his wife and two children. (He and Marie-Thérèse eventually had 13 children, only 3 of whom outlived their father.)

On June 4, 1701, Cadillac and his party left Montreal. There were 25 canoes in the expedition, carrying 50 soldiers and 50 settlers along with about 100 friendly Indians. Cadillac's nine-year-old son, Antoine, accompanied his father. For the next seven weeks, the settlers traveled from Montreal, up the Ottawa River to Lake Nipissing, down the French and Pickerel Rivers to Georgian Bay, and then south across the broad expanse of Lake Huron. From Lake Huron they entered the St. Clair River, which broadened into Lake St. Clair, then narrowed again to become the Detroit River, the strait that led to Lake Erie. On July 24, they landed at the present-day site of Detroit. Their journey covered about 600 miles and included at least 30 portages, places where canoes had to be carried overland.

Within just a few weeks, the 37-acre settlement was enclosed. Cadillac was charmed by the location of his city. "Its position is delightful and advantageous," he wrote about a year after the landing. "It is at the narrowest part of the river, where no one can pass by day without being seen." Still, life in Detroit was not easy. The village's streets were

In a letter to Louis Hector de Calliere (1646-1703), who succeeded Frontenac as governor general of New France, Cadillac claimed the Detroit River teemed with fish and that its banks were lined with trees and grape vines. Deer, turkey, pheasant, quail, and partridge were thick in the woods. "Can one believe that such a place where nature has given so much . . . will not yield to the worker . . . all that is desired?" he asked.

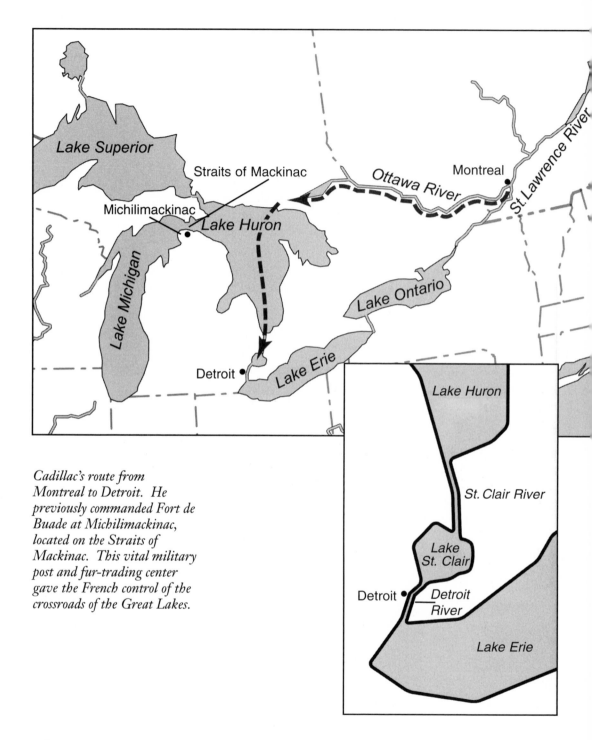

Cadillac's route from Montreal to Detroit. He previously commanded Fort de Buade at Michilimackinac, located on the Straits of Mackinac. This vital military post and fur-trading center gave the French control of the crossroads of the Great Lakes.

narrow. Building lots averaged just 25 feet across and 25 feet deep. Early houses were made of logs driven vertically into the ground, the spaces between them sealed with grass or mud. Floors were dirt, and roofs were made of bark or covered with skins. Many homes had no chimneys, so cooking was almost certainly done in communal kitchens. At first, there was no glass for windows or hinges for

A sketch of Detroit as it may have looked in 1701

doors. But living conditions improved as the population grew and land was cleared. As Cadillac had hoped, many groups of Indians were living nearby. Life became even more settled in the spring of 1702 when Cadillac's wife arrived in Detroit with their son Jacques. In those early years, Cadillac's family also grew. In 1704, Marie-Thérèse Cadillac was born, the first European child born in Detroit.

Upon landing at Detroit, Marie-Thérèse Cadillac is embraced by her husband, Antoine. The wife of Alphonse de Tonti, Cadillac's second in command, came as well. The two were the first European women in the area, and they traveled over 1,000 miles in open canoes to join their husbands.

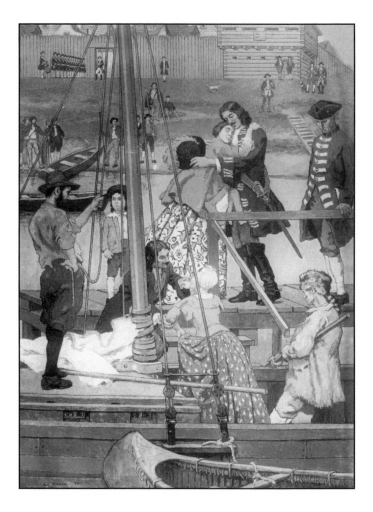

As leader of the settlement, Cadillac was in almost constant conflict with traders and merchants because of his efforts to monopolize trade. He also clashed with the Jesuits over governing power. The Jesuits had established most of the outposts in New France, and they wished to be in charge of the settlements. But Cadillac believed that "in matters pertaining to the civil state, the responsibility is mine, and I will decide what I think is in the King's best interest." On one occasion, he was called to Montreal, where he was arrested on charges of extortion and abuse of power. Ultimately, however, he was exonerated of those charges by the still-supportive Pontchartrain.

By 1707, however, reports of Cadillac's actions had raised serious questions even in the mind of Pontchartrain. François Clairambault d'Aigremont, a government inspector, was sent to investigate. Within a year, he completed a report that was to signal the beginning of the end of Cadillac's leadership of Detroit. In that report, Clairambault said that Cadillac was a profiteer who had lied about the growth of the settlement. He noted that Cadillac owned three times as much land as all the other settlers together. Cadillac's actions, he added, endangered France's hold on the Great Lakes region.

Even Pontchartrain could no longer support Cadillac. But neither could he turn against the man who had been his protégé. Instead, Pontchartrain appointed Cadillac governor of Louisiana in 1710. A year later, Cadillac left the northern reaches of New France, never to return. Behind him, however, he left

Sent to investigate Cadillac's administration of Detroit, François Clairambault dispatched a highly critical report back to France. This report read, in part: "Sieur de Lamothe is Detroit's largest landowner, alone having 157 arpents of improved land while all the others together have only 46 arpents. There are three cows, six or seven steers or calves and one horse; it would not be to sieur de Lamothe's advantage if there were more because he could not rent out his horse at ten livres a day if there were more animals." (An arpent is a measure of land slightly smaller than an acre. A livre is an old French coin originally equal to 16 ounces of silver.)

the sketchy beginnings of a great city. Although Detroit went through periods of trial, the settlement was instrumental in protecting French interests in North America for 60 years.

In Louisiana, Cadillac once again saw the enormous possibilities for trade. And, once again, he found himself at odds with officials of the colony and with the Native Americans. In 1716, Cadillac was recalled to France by the Ministry of Marine.

By late 1718, Cadillac had retired in St. Nicolas-de-la-Grave, the city of his birth. He applied for, and received, back salary he was owed for his service as governor of Louisiana. In recognition of his 30 years of service to the crown, he was awarded the Cross of St. Louis, making him a knight in this military order, and was paid all the salary arrears he claimed. In 1723, Cadillac used the proceeds from the sale of his property in Detroit to purchase the post of governor of the French town of Castelsarrasin. He served without distinction for seven years, and died there in October 1730.

Cadillac has been called one of the great heroes of the colonial period. He also has been called one of the greatest scoundrels ever to set foot in the territory the French called New France. In truth, while he was not motivated by religion or altruism as were several great founders of the New World, Cadillac was not unique. Many who came to settle in America were motivated by money, power, or adventure. Whether he was a hero or a scoundrel, Cadillac's accomplishments cannot be overlooked. He saw the strategic importance of Detroit and the potential to establish a great city where others saw only wilderness, and he acted courageously to make his dream a reality.

When residents of Detroit reenacted Cadillac's landing 300 years later in 2001, almost one million people lived in the city; another 4.5 million people lived in the metropolitan area. The city has been home to the American automobile industry for the past 100 years, and its fortune and population have ebbed and flowed with the car business. Detroit lost almost half its residents between 1950 and 2000, a decline fueled by urban problems and suburban growth. Detroit is likely to remain an important commercial center in the Midwest, however, because of its geographic location—a spot so carefully chosen by Antoine Cadillac many years ago.

Workers building cars on an early twentieth-century Ford Motor Company assembly line. General Motors, another Detroit automaker, named its luxury line of cars after Detroit's founder, Cadillac.

Michigan from Settlement to Statehood

In the years following the settlement of Detroit, the French continued to occupy Michigan, despite British attempts to move in and take over the lucrative fur trade. Control of the region changed after the British won the French and Indian War (1754-1763).

The British tried to develop friendly relations with the Native Americans of Michigan by passing a law in 1763 that made it virtually impossible for settlers to buy land from the natives. On the eve of the American Revolution, settlers and settlements were scarce in Michigan.

Nonetheless, Michigan became a bloody battleground. While some Native Americans sided with the rebels, most were friendly to the British. Detroit became a staging ground for British and Indian raids on the frontier settlements. Even after the Treaty of Paris (1783) ended the Revolutionary War, the British refused to cede Michigan and the rest of the Midwest to the United States. They were sure the fledgling country would not survive and wanted to maintain their profitable trade with the Indians. In 1794, the U.S. and Britain signed Jay's Treaty. One provision required Britain to end these violations of the Treaty of Paris, and the British left Michigan two years later.

The U.S. Congress, meanwhile, had anticipated the eventual British surrender of the western frontier regions. In 1787, it passed the Northwest Ordinance, establishing an orderly plan to divide the area north of the Ohio River and east of the Mississippi, called the Northwest Territory, into smaller territories that eventually would become three to five states.

On January 11, 1805, President Thomas Jefferson signed an act creating the Michigan Territory, an area that included the eastern tip of the present Upper Peninsula and all of the Lower Peninsula. A line drawn straight east through the southernmost tip of Lake Michigan marked the southern boundary at that time. About 4,000 settlers lived in the region.

During the War of 1812, fought by Britain and the U.S. from 1812 to 1815, Michigan became a focal point for military action on the western frontier. During the war, both Detroit and Mackinac Island fell to the British, not to be returned to American control until the end of the war. Following the war, the U.S. government purchased Michigan lands from the native people through a series of treaties. By 1842, the Indians had ceded all of their land, except for some small reserves.

Many of those treaties were negotiated by Lewis Cass, who served as territorial governor from 1813 through 1831. Cass attracted more settlers to the Michigan Territory by improving transportation. He encouraged the federal government to build military roads into the area. Steamships began sailing on the Great Lakes in 1818 and the Erie Canal was completed in 1825. Nationwide prosperity in the early 1830s boosted the population further because settlers had money to buy Michigan land. The territory's population, which was 31,640 in 1830, grew to more than 212,000 by 1840.

By 1834, Michigan had more than 60,000 residents, the minimum needed for statehood under the Northwest Ordinance of 1787. A boundary dispute between the Michigan and Ohio Territories, however, held up Michigan's request for statehood for several years. On January 26, 1837, with that dispute settled, Michigan became the 26th state.

The land fought over was the "Toledo Strip," the southern section of Michigan Territory. Michigan ceded the strip to Ohio and Indiana in exchange for the remainder of the Upper Peninsula. This proved to be a great deal, as the Upper Peninsula was filled with natural resources. Lumbermen made fortunes harvesting Michigan trees, and miners dug iron ore and copper found in the western part of the peninsula.

After serving as the territorial governor of Michigan, Lewis Cass (1782-1866) went on to become secretary of war (1831-1836) under President Andrew Jackson, and a U.S. senator representing Michigan (1845-1857). He was also the Democratic candidate for president in 1848.

Chapter Two

Charles Langlade
and the
Founding of Wisconsin

In June 1752, a group of 30 Ottawa and 180 Ojibwa warriors plus 30 French soldiers made their way by canoe from Michilimackinac to Detroit. From there the war party traveled to the Miami River in Ohio, then paddled to a landing spot near the Miami Indian village of Pickawillany, north of present-day Dayton, Ohio.

At that time, the French and British were supposed to be at peace. Instead, the two nations were engaged, as they had been for a century, in a violent struggle for control of the fur-rich lands in the interior of what would become the United States of America. The Native American warriors and French soldiers bound for Pickawillany were determined to establish French dominance in that part of the Ohio River valley.

This idealized likeness of Charles de Langlade (1729-1800) was designed for the Langlade County Historical Society by Sidney Bedore, one of Langlade's descendants.

Memeskia was known as
"Old Briton" because of his
fondness for the British.
The French called him *La
Demoiselle*, "the maiden," a
less flattering nickname.

In the mid-1600s, the
Miami occupied lands in
western Wisconsin,
northeastern Illinois, and
northern Indiana. The
Miami were hunters who
relied on buffalo to supply
most of their food and
clothing. By the time of
Langlade's birth, most of
the Miami had been driven
from their ancestral lands
to northwest Ohio by
invading Indians from the
north. They occupied this
area until the end of the
French and Indian War,
when they resettled in
Indiana. At that time there
were only about 1,700
members left in the tribe.

On the morning of June 21, the war party
came out of the thick forest that surrounded the
village and launched a surprise attack on the Miamis.
Most of the Indians who lived in the village were
gone on their summer hunt. Only a handful of
women remained, along with about two dozen
Miami warriors, their chief, Memeskia, and eight
British traders.

When the mixed group attacked Pickawillany,
screaming and firing their muskets, Miami women
working in the fields ran for the safety of a palisaded
fort at the center of the village. Several women and
three of the traders were trapped outside the fort
and killed. The remaining five traders and about
twenty Indians, including Memeskia, took refuge
inside the palisade. Their defense lasted only
through the afternoon. By the time the attack
ended, the village was in ashes, at least fourteen
Miami were dead, one British trader was stabbed to
death, and the remaining people were captured.
Memeskia himself met a fate not uncommon in
Native American warfare in those days. He was
killed and his body was boiled and eaten by the
attackers.

The man who led this bloody attack that put
the French in control of the Ohio River valley was a
23-year-old French-Ottawa officer named Charles
de Langlade. Langlade would go on to earn a justi-
fied reputation as a brave soldier, first in the service
of the French and later with the British in North
America. Eventually, he would become the first permanent settler in what is now Green Bay, Wisconsin.

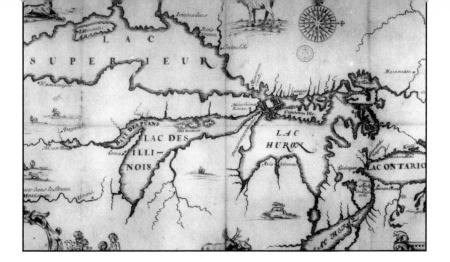

An early map of the Great Lakes region by French explorers. It includes the Baye des Puans, now Green Bay.

Wisconsin before Langlade

The first European known to have set foot on Wisconsin soil was Jean Nicolet, a French explorer. Like most of the early explorers of the upper Midwest region of the United States, Nicolet was searching for the fabled Northwest Passage when he arrived in 1634. Médard Chouart, sieur des Groseilliers, and his brother-in-law, Pierre Esprit Radisson, explored the Lake Superior area and spent the winters of 1659-1661 in northern Wisconsin.

During the next 15 years the Jesuits, a Roman Catholic religious order dedicated to missionary work, established the first missions, near present-day Ashland and De Pere. In 1673, the French fur trader Louis Joliet and Jesuit priest Jacques Marquette crossed Wisconsin by way of the Fox and Wisconsin Rivers to reach the Mississippi. These early European explorers encoun-

tered a number of Native American groups, including the Fox, Ioway, Kickapoo, Menominee, Miami, Ojibwa, Potawatomi, Sauk, Sioux, and Winnebago. All were descendants of the same Paleo-Indians and Archaic peoples who were the earliest inhabitants of the region.

The Europeans found a fertile land with thick forests, an abundance of game, and fish-filled lakes and streams. "The country was so pleasant, so beautiful & fruitfull," Radisson wrote. The lure of beaver and other fur-bearing animals whose pelts were in great demand in Europe enticed many fur trappers and traders into the area. In the late 1600s, several trading posts were established, including one at Prairie du Chien and another at Green Bay. It was many years, however, before any serious attempt was made to settle this frontier.

Langlade—whose full name was Charles-Michel Mouet de Langlade—was born in 1729. Though the exact date of his birth is not known, it was probably early May because he was baptized in the Roman Catholic faith on May 9. In those days when many infants died soon after birth, most Catholics living in the frontier wasted no time having their babies baptized.

Charles was the heir to a kind of frontier nobility. His father, Augustin de Langlade, was an important trader in the upper Great Lakes region the French called *pays d'en haut*. His mother was

These voyageurs camped for the night were part of the prosperous fur trade in the upper Great Lakes region, as was Augustin de Langlade.

the sister of Nissowaquet, a prominent Ottawa chief. Her Native American name is not known, but she took the name Domitilde when she became a Catholic sometime before Charles's birth. As the son of a Native American woman and a French man, Charles was reared as a *metis*, meaning "mixed." He moved easily between the French settlement at Michilimackinac, where he was educated in European ways by Jesuit priests, and the Indian villages of his Ottawa relatives, where he learned the ways of the forest.

At the age of 10, Charles was taken on a war party by his uncle Nissowaquet. His uncle had dreamed that the only way to conquer the enemy was for Charles to accompany him. Some accounts report the Ottawas won the battle against the Chickasaw Indians in Tennessee; others record that the two tribes negotiated a treaty. At the end of the raid, the boy was given the name Aukewingeketawso, or "military conqueror," by his Indian relatives. Around 1750, Charles married an Ottawa woman, Agathe, who was a member of Nissowaquet's band. Had Charles chosen to, he could easily have risen to a position of prominence among his mother's people. Instead, he opted to live his life as a *metis*, both French and Indian. In the process, he became a powerful presence in both the Indian and French colonial worlds.

In 1750, when he was about 21 years of age, Charles de Langlade enrolled in the French army's colonial service as a cadet. He seems to have soon proven his worth as a soldier, for just two years later

Pays d'en haut means "up country," which is how the French referred to the upper Great Lakes area of North America.

he was chosen to lead the expedition against the Pickawillany village.

The attack against the Miami people earned Langlade a degree of fame among both the French and the Native Americans on the frontier. That raid also helped shape what would be the last great conflict between the French and British in North America. As a consequence of the raid, the Miami and other tribes in the Ohio River valley turned their backs on alliances with the British, opting to fight on the side of the French.

Soon after the attack on Pickawillany, the French further tightened their hold on the Ohio River valley frontier by building three forts that barred British efforts to move into the valley. In response to the increased threat posed by the French and their Indian allies, in 1753 Governor Robert Dinwiddie of Virginia sent a young colonel named George Washington to the forts with a demand that the French leave the frontier. The French, in a position of strength, replied that they planned to drive every Englishman from the Ohio River valley.

Anxious to wrest control of the land from the French, Dinwiddie's immediate response to the French refusal to abandon the valley was to order the construction of a British fort. Built on the site of present-day Pittsburgh, Pennsylvania, where the Monongahela and Allegheny Rivers meet the Ohio, that fort was almost immediately captured by French colonial soldiers and their Indian comrades and named Fort Duquesne in honor of the Marquis Abraham Duquesne, governor of New France (Canada).

Top: Robert Dinwiddie (1693-1770), governor of colonial Virginia; bottom: George Washington (1732-1799) as a young soldier

As a consequence, Great Britain ordered two regiments—around 1,400 soldiers—to America, under the command of Major General Sir Edward Braddock. About 400 members of the colonial militia were added to the force, and Braddock led the small army from Virginia to the Ohio River, cutting a road as they marched to Fort Duquesne.

In the summer of 1755, the French became aware that Braddock was leading his small army toward the fort. Langlade, by that time an ensign in the French colonial service, was called to action again. He joined a group of about 850, many of whom were Native American warriors, led by Lienard de Beaujeu. On July 18, in the forest about seven miles from the fort, the French and Native Americans ambushed Braddock and his men. After Beaujeu was killed, Langlade led the group. The British officers were on horseback and easily picked off; the foot soldiers, trained to shoot in volleys on command, were unprepared to fight an enemy hidden among the trees. The British were completely routed. More than half of Braddock's men were killed or wounded. Braddock himself was shot and died a few days after the battle. Braddock's crushing defeat in what came to be known as the Battle of the Wilderness was one of the defining moments of the French and Indian War. It delayed the ultimate British victory for control of the frontier for several years.

A volley is a number of bullets or missiles discharged at the same time.

The British credited Langlade for the French success. As a result of his actions at Pickawillany and in the defeat of Braddock, Langlade was suddenly famous on the French frontier, in Quebec, the

capital of New France, and even at Versailles, the palace of the French King Louis XIV. Meanwhile, after Braddock's defeat, the major action in the war shifted north, to the St. Lawrence River valley and the Canadian cities of Montreal and Quebec. By late 1757, Langlade and his Indian comrades had joined the fighting along the St. Lawrence River.

Charles Langlade (left, arm raised) directed the attack of Indians from Wisconsin and Michigan. In the background, General Edward Braddock falls off his horse, while George Washington, a major in the colonial militia, catches the horse's bridle.

43

The French and Indian Wars

The French and Indian Wars were a series of conflicts fought in North America between 1689 and 1763 as France and Great Britain struggled for control of the vast interior of what became the United States and the region's rich fur trade. In each of the four wars, both sides fought with the support of Native American allies.

The first, King William's War, consisted mostly of frontier attacks on the British colonies from 1689 to 1697. Queen Anne's War (1702-1713) and King George's War (1744-1748) were linked to wars in Europe. The last and most important conflict in this bloody struggle was the French and Indian War, waged from 1754 until 1763. Though this war broke out in North America, it soon spread to Europe, where it was called the Seven Years' War.

The conflict centered on rights to the Ohio River valley. The British and French both claimed the region. When the governor of New France sent a force to construct and hold posts in Ohio and Pennsylvania, the American colonists and British fought to oust them. The battles then headed north through upstate New York and into New France (Canada). The French and Indian War ended soon after the French strongholds of Montreal and Quebec fell to Great Britain.

In 1763, with the signing of the Treaty of Paris, Great Britain controlled all French land in Canada along with all of France's holdings east of the Mississippi River except New Orleans. Great Britain also received the territory of Florida from Spain, which had become France's ally in 1762. The conclusion of the war marked the end of the French government's meaningful presence in North America and set the stage for the rapid westward expansion of the American colonies.

A military unit struggles up the Allegheny Mountains during the French and Indian War.

During the next several years, Langlade and the Indians who followed him into battle were a force to be reckoned with. At home in the deep forests, they were particularly adept at finding and attacking British scouting parties. In January 1758, Langlade led his men in an ambush that turned back a raid by the famous frontier fighter Robert Rogers and his Rangers near Lake Champlain in Vermont.

As the tide of war swung in favor of the British, and the French began losing control of their extensive lands in the New World in the years between 1759 and 1761, Langlade continued to fight for the French. He took part in the siege of Quebec and fought at Montreal until he was ordered to leave not long before that city fell to the British in 1760. From Montreal, Langlade made his way to Michilimackinac, where he served as second in command until that post, too, fell to the British in October 1760.

By this time Langlade could see the French were fighting in a losing cause. Like many other French frontiersmen, he transferred his loyalty to the British. Langlade quickly adjusted to life under British rule. In the period from late 1761 until early 1763, he lived in Michilimackinac, making occasional trading voyages.

In 1763, Ottawa chief Pontiac organized a Native American alliance that included almost all the tribes in the Ohio River valley and Great Lakes area. Pontiac led an attack against Detroit. He might have succeeded if his plan to take the fort had not been betrayed by informers. Following this

Born in Massachusetts, Robert Rogers (1731-1795) fought on the side of the British during the French and Indian War. A versatile leader, he commanded a guerrilla company, Rogers's Rangers, that gained fame as a group of ferocious, stealthy, and merciless fighters. Rogers fought for the British again during the Revolutionary War.

Chief Pontiac met with Britain's Major Henry Gladwin before the Ottawa surrounded the fort at Detroit.

A siege is when an army attempts to take over a place by surrounding it and stopping goods and people from going in and out.

aborted effort to directly capture the fort, Pontiac besieged Detroit, an effort that lasted five months. He lifted the siege when the French and British signed a peace treaty, removing all hope of French aid to his cause.

Under Pontiac's leadership, however, the tribes in the alliance captured 10 of the 14 British military posts in the wilderness that stretched from

Pennsylvania to the Mississippi River. The fort at Michilimackinac was among the ones taken by Indians, with the loss of many lives. Langlade has been credited with using his influence with the Native Americans to save the lives of British commander George Etherington and several others.

By the end of Pontiac's War in 1765, Langlade had moved to the site of present-day Green Bay, Wisconsin. He took with him his father and mother, his wife, Charlotte, and their two daughters. Both he and his father had probably lived there previously for short periods. But this time, they intended to stay.

Green Bay had long been visited by French explorers and trappers. The famous French explorer Jean Nicolet arrived first in 1634 while he was seeking a water route to the Pacific Ocean. About 45 years later, in 1679, another famous explorer, René Robert Cavelier, sieur de La Salle, sailed into the bay with his men aboard their ship, the *Griffon*. In the years following La Salle's visit, the location became a French fur-trading post and mission.

The Langlades established a trading post at the place they called La Baye. Charles flourished as a trader and lived a comfortable life with his wife and family. This peaceful existence in Green Bay was interrupted with the onset of the Revolutionary War in 1776. At this time, Langlade joined forces with the British to fight against the patriots who wanted to free the 13 American colonies from British rule. Langlade saw action in Montreal and in what was then the western frontier, defending Vincennes, Indiana, in 1779 from American forces under the

Back at Michilimackinac, in 1754 Charles de Langlade met and married Charlotte Bourassa, daughter of a wealthy trader at the straits. Although Langlade abandoned Agathe, his first wife, he did educate their son, Charles Jr., sending him to school in Montreal.

Jean Nicolet (1598-1642) was searching for a water route through North America to the Orient when he landed in Green Bay in 1634 (above). Nicolet wore a Chinese robe because he was expecting to see Orientals. Instead he met a small group of Menominee, who were impressed by Nicolet and prepared a feast in his honor. La Salle's ship, the Griffon (below), arrived later, in 1679. The ship anchored offshore, while La Salle's men loaded furs into a small boat that returned to the Griffon.

command of George Rogers Clark. He also led a failed attempt to wrest what is now St. Louis, Missouri, from the control of the Spanish, who were then allied with the American patriots.

Following the war, Langlade returned to his life of comfort and fur trading in Green Bay. The British (who continued to control Wisconsin until 1794, even though they lost the war) granted him land in Green Bay and in Canada as well as a lifelong annuity equal to half his pay as a soldier. As he grew older, he apparently enjoyed talking about what he claimed were 99 different battles during his long and active life. In fact, a placard placed where Langlade's home stood near the Fox River reads: "Charles de Langlade 'Bravest of the Brave' Led His Indian Band in Ninety-Nine Battles. His Tact and Diplomacy Brought Peace to the Warring Tribes along the Fox River. He was Held in High Esteem By French, English and Americans." One witness said Langlade often lamented that his life as a soldier was ending. "I wish there would be one more foray in which I could take part to make it 100 [battles]," he reportedly said before his death in 1800.

Green Bay was dominated by a few powerful trapping and trading families, such as Langlade's, until the end of the War of 1812. During that war, the British had retaken the area. Afterwards, American troops were stationed at Green Bay, building Fort Howard in 1816. Americans eager to mine, farm, and cut timber soon followed the soldiers. These pioneers replaced the trapper-trader way of life that Langlade and others with a foot in both the

Native Americans canoe and fish in the bay in front of Fort Howard.

Indian and French cultures had forged in the *pays d'en haut*.

Incorporated as a city in 1854, today this port of 100,000 people still depends on Lake Michigan for two important industries: fishing and tourism. Green Bay is perhaps best known, however, for its public ownership of a National Football League team, the Green Bay Packers. Passionate Packers fans have cheered the team on to 12 championship victories since its first season in 1919, more titles than any other NFL team has won.

Wisconsin from Settlement to Statehood

Although the British were to have passed control of Wisconsin to the United States at the end of the American Revolution, this was not done until 1794. Even then, the British continued to control the rich fur trade in the region because of their dominant position in nearby Canada.

During the War of 1812, Wisconsin once again fell into British hands. After winning the war, however, the U.S. regained control and Wisconsin became part of the Illinois Territory. A few years later, in 1818, present-day Wisconsin became part of the Michigan Territory. In the 1820s, the discovery of lead in southwest Wisconsin brought a rush of miners into the region. This was followed by a second wave of settlers eager to farm Wisconsin's lush land.

During the early years of settlement, the U.S. Army played a major role in the region, protecting settlements by establishing forts at strategic locations, including Green Bay, and building bridges, trails, and roads throughout the region. Not surprisingly, the Native Americans grew angry about the presence of more and more settlers and their insatiable demands for land. In 1832, this anger resulted in Black Hawk's War, fought by the Sauk and Fox Indians and other allied tribes against the white settlers. This revolt was brutally crushed and proved to be the last real Native American resistance in the area.

In 1836, Wisconsin was made a territory in its own right. By 1840, population in the territory had risen to more than 130,000. Conflicts over claims to land near Chicago and the Upper Peninsula of Michigan, however, kept the area from achieving statehood until 1848. On May 30 of that year, Wisconsin became the 30th state of the Union.

Black Hawk's Indian name was Ma-ka-tai-me-she-kia-kiak, or Black Sparrow Hawk. White Americans shortened it to Black Hawk.

52

Chapter Three

Jean du Sable
the
Forgotten Founder of Chicago

Sometimes men and women who should be famous because of their exploits are overlooked, their accomplishments lost in the shadows of the distant past. For many years, this was the fate of Jean Baptiste Pointe du Sable, the first settler in what eventually became the great city of Chicago, Illinois. Indeed, for most of the last 200 years, another man—a trader named John Kinzie—was honored as Chicago's founder.

Once du Sable had been rediscovered, historians faced the task of separating legends from facts. They weren't even sure how his name was spelled. In records and documents that have survived the centuries since he trapped and traded in the area around Chicago, he is also referred to as de Sable, Pointe de Sable, Au Sable, Sabre, and Pointe de Saible.

This likeness of Jean Baptiste Pointe du Sable (1745?-1818?) was made by engraver Charles C. Dawson.

Most accounts agree that Jean Baptiste was born in 1745 (or perhaps 1750) in San Marc, Haiti. His mother was a slave woman of African descent whose name is unknown. His father was French, either a sea captain or possibly a member of the Dandonneau family, well-known French settlers who were active in the North American fur trade. (Some Dandonneaus added the title Sieur du Sable to their name.) Du Sable was usually described as a black man, and he called himself a "free negro."

Some historians speculate that du Sable attended school in Paris at some time during his youth. As evidence that he was educated, these scholars point to the facts that at one time he may have owned several oil paintings and that he was a successful businessman. Documentary evidence shows, however, that du Sable only initialed documents, rather than signing them, casting doubt that he received any formal education.

According to one of the most repeated stories, Jean du Sable left Haiti in late 1763 or early 1764 on board the sloop *Susanne*, perhaps owned by his father. The ship was bound for Louisiana, at the time a Spanish territory, and may have been shipwrecked near the Louisiana coast. Du Sable feared being thought a runaway slave and may also have been injured, according to some, but fortunately a group of Jesuit priests in New Orleans took him in. Then, in 1765, he made a 600-mile journey by canoe up the Mississippi River to St. Louis, Missouri. On this journey, du Sable was accompanied by Jacques Clamorgan, a trader and merchant who went on to become one of the first judges of the Court of Common Pleas in St. Louis. Some versions claim du Sable was also accompanied by a Potawatomi Indian named Choctaw, whom he had met at the mission in New Orleans.

Whichever adventures he really experienced, Jean du Sable did arrive in the northwest frontier, where he became the owner of 800 acres of farmland in central Illinois, near what is now the city of Peoria. Du Sable stayed in Peoria until 1779, when he relocated to the land the Potawatomi Indians called *Checagou* in northeast Illinois. There he soon established a house and trading post on the banks of the Chicago River, near the heart of what is now the great city's downtown.

Illinois before du Sable

The French explorers who first came to the Illinois Country, as it was known in the seventeenth and eighteenth centuries, found the land inhabited by several groups of native people. The earliest explorers came in contact with the Illinois, a confederation of Algonquian-speaking people that included the Cahokia, Kaskaskia, Michigamea, Moingwena, Peoria, and Tamaroa tribes. As the fur trade grew stronger, Iroquois Indians moved into Illinois, along with Fox, Sauk, Kickapoo, and Potawatomi.

For more than a century following the earliest exploration of Illinois, the region remained a wilderness peopled only by Native Americans and by a few French trappers and soldiers. By the time Jean du Sable arrived in Chicago, the Potawatomi were the most powerful tribe in the region. Potawatomi meant "Fire Nation." They dominated a large territory spreading from Wisconsin to Michigan, including much of northern Illinois and Indiana.

The land on which du Sable settled had long been known to European explorers. Father Jacques Marquette and Louis Joliet, explorer and mapmaker, were the first Europeans to visit when they passed the site on their return from exploring the Mississippi River in 1673. Many other trappers and explorers followed in their footsteps in the years after their famous journey, including Robert La Salle in 1679 and Henri Joutel in 1687-1688. But no one, it seemed, wanted to stay in *Checagou*.

It was not until 1696 that the Europeans made any serious attempt to establish a presence in the region. At that time, Father François Pinet, a Jesuit missionary, founded the Mission of the Guardian Angel to serve two Miami villages not far from present-day Chicago. This mission was abandoned in 1700 when the priest's efforts to convert the Native Americans to Christianity proved fruitless.

During the years from 1700 until du Sable appeared on the scene, the site was little more than a spot where Indians and European fur trappers could portage their canoes. Several explorers, including the great La Salle, recognized the importance of the *Checagou* plain because of its role as a portage leading to the Illinois River, which empties into the Mississippi. Yet Europeans did not establish a permanent foothold in the region.

Du Sable seems to have had good relations with the Indians who lived near Chicago. He married a Potawatomi woman whom he called Catherine. The couple had two children, a daughter, Susanne, and a son, named Jean Baptiste like his father.

Perhaps the early Europeans who visited the *Checagou* plain were driven off by the way the land smelled, since many historians believe *Checagou*, sometimes also spelled *Eschecagou*, is a Potawatomi word that means either "skunk" or "wild onion." Other historians, it should be noted, believe the word was a reference to something "large" or "great," though no one knows for sure why it would be used to describe the empty plain on which Chicago was eventually created.

Louis Joliet and Jacques Marquette

Louis Joliet was born in 1645 and educated—first in a Jesuit Seminary in Quebec and later in France—in preparation for the priesthood. In 1668, upon his return to New France (Canada), he abandoned his plans to become a priest and became a trader among the Native Americans.

In 1669, he met Père (Father) Jacques Marquette. Born in 1637 in Laon, France, Marquette was a Jesuit missionary who came to the New World in 1666. After studying Indian languages and training in Trois-Rivières for about 18 months, he traveled west across Lake Huron and founded a mission at Sault Saint Marie, Michigan, in 1668. He also served at La Pointe, Wisconsin, from 1669 to 1671, and then when the Hurons and Ottawas moved, he returned to the Straits of Mackinac to establish a mission at Point Saint Ignace (now St. Ignace, Michigan).

Louis de Buade, comte de Frontenac, governor of New France, commissioned Joliet and Marquette to explore and chart the Mississippi River. Setting sail from Point Saint Ignace in May 1673 with five companions, they crossed Lake Michigan to Green Bay, Wisconsin. From there, they paddled upstream along the Fox River and then, after a portage, descended the Wisconsin River. On June 17, 1673, the party entered the Mississippi River, becoming the first Europeans to do so. They then followed the Mississippi southward to a point below the mouth of the Arkansas River before turning back.

On their return journey north they traveled through the center of the state, up the Illinois River. On this journey, they portaged their small boats between the Des Plaines River, a tributary of the Illinois River, and the Chicago River, which flowed into Lake Michigan. The Chicago portage, as it was later called, became an important link in the trade route between the Great Lakes and the Mississippi River.

Marquette remained at Lake Michigan, returning to his missionary work among the Illinois Indians until his death in 1675. Joliet went on to Quebec to report on their journey of exploration. Joliet continued exploring, becoming one of the first Europeans to visit Labrador and Hudson Bay. He died in 1700.

Jacques Marquette and Louis Joliet on their historic Mississippi River voyage (above). Robert de La Salle (right) reached the mouth of the Mississippi in 1682.

René Robert Cavelier, sieur de La Salle

Born in 1643 in Rouen, France, and educated by Jesuit priests, La Salle was perhaps the most famous French explorer in North America. In 1666, he immigrated to Canada and became a trader. Soon, he turned his attention to exploring the world unseen by Europeans, first visiting the region south of Lakes Ontario and Erie, and, it is thought, becoming the first European to see the Ohio River.

Because of his ability to speak Native American languages and his familiarity with the wilderness, he was named the commander of Fort Frontenac in Kingston, Ontario, on Lake Ontario, near the head of the St. Lawrence River.

In 1677, he visited France, where he obtained royal approval for a plan to explore the Mississippi River. Returning with explorer Henry de Tonty, he spent several years exploring the Great Lakes and establishing forts, including one along the Illinois River in Illinois. In 1681, he and Tonty, along with a party of French and Native Americans, began an epic journey down the Mississippi River, reaching the Gulf of Mexico in April 1682. During his journey, La Salle claimed all the land south of Illinois to the Gulf of Mexico and west from the Mississippi to Spanish territories for Louis XIV, king of France, and named the region Louisiana.

In 1684, after a visit to France, La Salle set out with a fleet of four ships on an expedition to establish a colony at the mouth of the Mississippi River. When the explorer and his men reached the Gulf of Mexico, however, they sailed past the Mississippi and landed on the shore of what is now Matagorda Bay, Texas. La Salle searched in vain for the mouth of the river before finally realizing his mistake. In January 1687, he and 17 men set out for Canada in an attempt to get help for the few members of the original expedition still left alive on the shore of Matagorda Bay. During this overland journey, La Salle's men mutinied, or rebelled, and he was killed.

Evidence shows that du Sable lived well during his time in Chicago. He enlarged and improved his home until it became more of a frontier mansion than a log cabin. His dwelling was 40 feet long and 22 feet wide. It had a piazza, or porch, running along the front, a parlor with a huge stone fireplace, a kitchen, and two sleeping rooms. Each room had at least one window, which was kept covered with tanned deerskin on cold nights. The structure also had slate floors and a slate roof. It was furnished

In 1779, Chicago consisted of du Sable's cabin at the mouth of the Chicago River, where it emptied into Lake Michigan.

with bearskin rugs and furniture built by du Sable using logs from the nearby forest.

In addition to the main cabin, du Sable built several outbuildings, including two large barns, a bakehouse, a poultry house, a workshop, a dairy, and a smokehouse. He must have grown wheat and corn, because he also had a millhouse where a horse-driven millstone ground grain into flour. An inventory of tools and other items at the homesite—taken when du Sable sold the property in 1800—included eight axes, several saws, carpenter's tools, seven scythes, eight sickles, three carts, and a plow. This inventory suggests that du Sable must have had a considerable number of employees, probably Potawatomi Indians. One man—who was frequently gone on trading journeys—would not have needed so many tools. Still on file in the Wayne County Court House in Detroit, the inventory also states that du Sable owned 11 copper kettles and a large French walnut cabinet with four glass doors.

A trader who met du Sable while in Chicago described him as a "large man; a trader, and pretty wealthy."

During the years that the American colonies were fighting to gain independence from Great Britain (1775-1783), the Midwest frontier was the site of several fierce battles between colonial troops led by George Rogers Clark and their British opponents. While it appears that du Sable sympathized with the British, in the summer of 1779 he was arrested by a troop of British soldiers. Charged with carrying on treasonable trade with the enemy—probably some of Clark's rebel soldiers—he was taken under guard to Mackinac Island, located in Lake Huron, near the straits. According to a

Historians wonder what du Sable might have kept in his walnut cabinet. There were no books or china listed on the inventory.

The fort on Mackinac Island, where Jean du Sable was held, was built high on a hill.

Lieutenant Thomas Bennett, who led the detail that arrested him, du Sable was a gentleman who had "many friends who give him a good character."

At about the same time that Jean du Sable was taken to Mackinac Island, the commander of the post there—Colonel Arent Schuyler de Peyster— was transferred to command the British post at Detroit. He was replaced by Lieutenant-Governor Patrick Sinclair. Though du Sable was a prisoner when he first met the new commander at Mackinac, he impressed Sinclair so much that Sinclair put him in charge of a large trading establishment he owned on the St. Clair River, just a few miles south of present-day Port Huron, Michigan.

For the next four years, until sometime in 1784, du Sable worked at this establishment, known as "The Pinery." The documentary record still in existence includes an inventory of du Sable's personal effects while he was at The Pinery. Included in this inventory is a list of some 23 paintings. It is this list, along with testimony of de Peyster that du Sable was "well educated," that has led some historians to believe that du Sable went to school in France. It seems likely, however, that these paintings were, in fact, the property of Sinclair, who owned The Pinery and all its contents.

In 1784, at the end of the Revolutionary War, du Sable returned to Chicago. Thanks to increasing trade in the Great Lakes region, the trader quickly built a thriving business. He supplied his customers with pork, bread, and flour (all of which he produced himself) in exchange for other goods or cash. He continued to live in harmony with his Native American neighbors and, over the years, built a reputation as a man of character.

In May 1800, Jean Baptiste Point du Sable sold his property in Chicago to a trader, Jean la Lime. One of the witnesses to this transaction was John Kinzie, the man credited with being the founder of Chicago. Kinzie himself bought du Sable's home in 1804. Exactly why du Sable sold his Chicago property where he had prospered is another mystery.

Although he was not the founder of Chicago, John Kinzie (1763-1828) was an important man in the city's early history. He operated a trading post and soon virtually every business in the fast-growing frontier settlement was under Kinzie's control.

"The first white man who settled here [in Chicago] was a Negro," wrote Juliette Augusta Magill Kinzie (1806-1870), the wife of John Kinzie, about du Sable.

Perhaps he was unhappy about the increasing number of settlers who were moving into the frontier in the wake of the Revolutionary War. Some sources say he failed in a bid to become a Potawatomi chief. Others say his wife died, although it is quite possible that she lived a few years after the move.

In any event, du Sable returned to Peoria, where he lived until 1805, when he moved to St. Charles, Missouri. There he purchased some farmland and lived with his son, Jean Baptiste. By mid-1813, du Sable, then probably 68 years old, was obviously concerned about his future. At that time, he transferred ownership of his house and land in St. Charles, along with some other property, to his granddaughter, Eulalie Baroda Derais. In exchange for the land, Eulalie promised to care for him for the rest of his life and to bury him in the Roman Catholic cemetery in St. Charles upon his death.

In February 1814, Jean Baptiste Point du Sable Jr. died. By September, du Sable Sr. was imprisoned in the St. Charles jail, apparently for indebtedness. There is a record that he applied to the court to take advantage of laws allowing some debtors lenient treatment.

That is the last reference to du Sable in the historical record. His death date is often given as 1818—the same year Illinois became a state. It can only be hoped that he was able to obtain his freedom and that his granddaughter Eulalie did, indeed, care for him as his long and exciting life came to an end.

The record of du Sable's life is sketchy, yet it paints the portrait of a brave, enterprising, and intelligent man. He inspired friendships among the British and French as well as among the Native Americans around Chicago. He was a pioneer in the true sense of the word, a man who made his way into the wilderness, where he established a foothold that grew to be one of the greatest cities in the world.

Chicago's first growth spurt followed the opening of the Erie Canal in 1825, only seven years after du Sable's death. The canal made travel to Illinois easier. Chicago was chartered as a city in 1837.

Farmers of the fertile prairie that surrounds the city sent their grain and livestock to Chicago. Meatpacking became a major industry in the mid-1800s.

Then in 1871, fire destroyed one-third of the city. About 17,000 buildings burned and 250 people were killed. Many of the rebuilt structures were made of steel and glass instead of wood. New construction materials and techniques now made tall buildings possible. For years Chicago competed against New York City to erect the biggest skyscraper and won in 1974, when the 1,454-foot Sears Tower was completed. The Sears Tower was the tallest building in the world for more than 20 years and in 2003 remained the tallest in the United States.

The first of many shipments of Illinois wheat was sent from Chicago in 1838.

The Sears Tower surrounded by other skyscrapers in downtown Chicago

As its early history suggested, Chicago became a transportation hub of the Midwest. In 2003, it was the second busiest port on the Great Lakes, a major railroad and trucking hub, and a center of air transport, with three airports. Almost three million people called Chicago home in the early twenty-first century; a total of nine million lived in the metropolitan area.

The busiest Great Lakes port (ranked according to tons shipped) was the harbor shared by Duluth, Minnesota, and Superior, Wisconsin.

Illinois from Settlement to Statehood

Under the terms of the Treaty of Paris of 1783, which ended the American Revolution, Great Britain surrendered the region including Illinois to the United States. In 1787, this vast region was organized as the Northwest Territory. In 1800, Illinois was made part of the Indiana Territory, then later organized as a separate territory. The Illinois Territory contained not only present-day Illinois, but also most of Wisconsin and large parts of Michigan and Minnesota.

White settlement proceeded slowly in Illinois during the early nineteenth century and was concentrated in the southern regions of the territory. The first settlement in northern Illinois developed around Fort Dearborn, the fort built in 1803 near du Sable's trading post in Chicago.

One of the reasons settlers did not rush to the rich lands in Illinois was that Native Americans in the region resisted their coming. While the territorial government had obtained land from the inhabitants through

Native Americans attack soldiers at Fort Dearborn during the War of 1812.

Erected in 1803, old Fort Dearborn was destroyed during the War of 1812.

a series of treaties, the Fox, Kickapoo, Potawatomi, and Sauk quickly became dissatisfied with their land agreements.

During the War of 1812, when Britain and the United States again took up arms, many of the Indians fought on the side of the British. In August 1812, they burned Fort Dearborn and killed about half the soldiers and residents, taking the rest as prisoners. Following that war, the Potawatomi sold their lands to the U.S. government. Most of them were moved west, first to a reservation in southern Kansas, and from there to Oklahoma in 1868. (In 1990, almost 17,000 people in the United States claimed to be descendants of members of the Potawatomi tribe.)

Fort Dearborn was rebuilt by 1817. With the war and resistance from the Native Americans over, the number of white settlers moving into the territory increased. Thousands of emigrants from Virginia, Kentucky, and other southern states traveled by flatboat and barge down the Ohio River to settle in Illinois. Other pioneers traveled by wagon across the Allegheny Mountains. Most of the new-comers settled in the wooded areas of southern Illinois, which were similar to the eastern and southern states from which they came. The vast, sparsely wooded prairies of central and northern Illinois were settled later.

On December 3, 1818, Illinois became the 21st state of the Union. Kaskaskia became the state capital. The capital was moved to Vandalia in 1820, and finally to Springfield in 1839.

Chapter Four

———— ◆ ————

George Rogers Clark
and the
Opening of Indiana

———— ◆ ————

I n February 1779, during the midst of the Revolutionary War, a force of about 170 men slogged through the hardwood forest and marshy wetlands of southwest Indiana. This ragtag army, comprised of Kentucky woodsmen and French militiamen, was bound for Vincennes, an important frontier outpost that they hoped to seize from the British.

Under the command of a 26-year-old former surveyor and frontier guide named George Rogers Clark, this small force would ultimately take control not only of Vincennes, but also of the entire north-west frontier. Thanks to this victory, a vast expanse of land that includes what is now Ohio, Indiana, and Illinois was kept out of British hands. During peace negotiations at the end of the Revolutionary War,

Reported to be a tall, handsome man, George Rogers Clark (1752-1818) was a charismatic leader who people willingly followed.

this large area—known as the Northwest Territory—was ceded to the United States by the British.

Clark received little credit for his accomplishments in his lifetime. In fact, he died a near pauper and a largely forgotten man. Today, however, Clark is famous as the "conqueror of the Northwest," one of the brave shapers of America who helped make the settlement of the midwestern United States possible.

Born on November 19, 1752, George Rogers Clark was the second son of John Clark and Ann Rogers Clark. Descended from Scottish immigrants, his parents were planters in Albemarle County, Virginia, not far from the birthplace of Thomas Jefferson. It is unclear whether George received any formal education as a boy. Through journals he wrote later in his life, we know he was a capable writer, indicating that he had some formal schooling or that he was educated at home. This homeschooling was not at all unusual on the frontier.

Wherever George went to school, he undoubtedly spent much of his free time in the woods of rural Virginia. He would have learned to hunt, trap, and fish at an early age and was probably comfortable on horseback even as a small boy.

In 1770, when George was 18, his younger brother, William, was born. William Clark would later gain fame as a leader of the Corps of Discovery expedition that would explore the Louisiana Territory. At about the same time William was born, George began learning surveying from his maternal grandfather, John Rogers.

A Clark family legend contended that members with red hair distinguished themselves in life. George was born with red hair; so was his brother William.

William Clark

Born in 1770, William Clark was the younger brother of George Rogers Clark. Like his older brother, he decided as a young man to find success as a soldier. In 1789 he joined a militia company and soon became an infantry officer in the army of General Anthony Wayne, who was then attempting to drive Native American people from the Ohio River valley. William Clark soon gained a reputation for leadership and courage. It was at this time that William first met Meriwether Lewis, when Lewis served briefly in Clark's rifle company.

In June 1803, Lewis asked Clark to join him on an expedition, commissioned by U.S. president Thomas Jefferson, to explore the newly purchased Louisiana Territory all the way to the Pacific Ocean.

As commanding officers of the Corps of Discovery, Lewis and Clark divided lead-ership responsibilities. William Clark was the expedition's mapmaker as well as its leading negotiator with Native American people. Their successful two-year trek to the Pacific and back made Clark a famous and influential man. Only one man was lost on the journey and much information about this new land was gained.

In 1807, Clark was appointed agent for the tribes west of the Mississippi River. He later took part in treaty negotia-tions with the western Indians following the War of 1812. From 1813 to 1821, he served as governor of the Missouri Territory. From 1821 until his death in 1838, he acted again as Indian agent. Following Meriwether Lewis's death in 1809, William Clark took over the job of completing a report about their famous expedition. Published in 1814, this report remains a classic of American history.

In 1763, King George III of Great Britain had issued a proclamation to his American subjects, prohibiting colonial expansion into the lands that lay west of the Appalachian Mountains. (The king and his ministers were profiting from the fur trade and hoped to protect it from competition.) Despite the king's order, many young Virginians were crossing the mountains into Kentucky in search of land and adventure. In 1772, Clark became one of those young men, leaving home to look for fame and fortune. Packing his surveying instruments and a geometry book, he journeyed to Fort Pitt (now the city of Pittsburgh, Pennsylvania), where he boarded a flatboat that carried him down the Ohio River.

During the next several years, Clark used his surveying skills to locate land for himself about 40 miles south of what is now Wheeling, West Virginia. He also staked claims for members of his family and other Virginia settlers who wanted to move west. Eventually, he became a guide for settlers.

In May 1775, George Rogers Clark made his way into Kentucky for the first time. The land was beautiful, but in turmoil. Several different land companies claimed the right to sell sections. The Native Americans, resentful of settlers who were taking what had long been their hunting lands, harassed the Kentucky pioneers. In June of the next year, Clark called a meeting in Harrodsburg, Kentucky, of representatives of all the "forts," as the walled frontier settlements were called. He and another delegate, John Gabriel Jones, were dispatched to Williamsburg, Virginia, to try to have Kentucky

A mural illustrating Clark's entrance into Kentucky

recognized—and therefore protected—as a county of Virginia. Governor Patrick Henry, who would later win fame for his "give me liberty or give me death" speech, gave Clark 500 pounds of gunpowder for the Kentuckians to use in their war with the Native Americans. At the same time, Virginia's General Assembly voted to make Kentucky a part of Virginia.

The fact that Clark was able to sway Henry and the other Virginians to his point of view says a great deal about his abilities as a speaker and a leader. Only 24 years of age when he was sent to Williamsburg, Clark was well over six feet tall and, according to contemporary accounts, was ruggedly handsome, with flaming red hair. Men who served under him in battle—the men who knew him best— were almost without exception willing to follow him wherever he led.

Patrick Henry (1736-1799) delivers his famous speech on the rights of the colonies before the Virginia Assembly.

In 1777, the Indian assaults that Clark had predicted two years earlier began. Thanks to his foresight, the settlements on the frontier were armed and ready when virtually all the tribes of the Ohio region—the Miami, Shawnee, and Wyandot—began a series of attacks. The Native Americans were aided by the British, who had recruited them as allies during the Revolutionary War, which began in 1775.

By that time, Clark had been made a major in Virginia's militia. He was in charge of all Kentucky's defenses. Unwilling to simply sit behind a palisade waiting for the Indians to attack, he decided to raid British outposts in the west, hoping this would disrupt the flow of supplies that were being sent to the Indians. He chose as his targets the forts at Kaskaskia in what is now Illinois and Vincennes on the Wabash River in what is now Indiana.

These forts were under the control of Henry Hamilton, the lieutenant governor of Canada. The American colonists hated Hamilton, whom they called the "hair buyer" because he not only supplied the Indians for battle, but also paid them for scalps they brought to his headquarters in Detroit.

After learning from spies that the forts at Vincennes and Kaskaskia were minimally protected by British troops, Clark devised a daring plan. He would take one company (leaving the rest to defend Kentucky settlements) across 450 miles of wilderness and attack the forts. No one, neither the British nor their allies, expected such an attack from Kentucky.

The Shawnee first lived in Ohio, but were driven into the South by the Iroquois. Some settled in Tennessee, but were pushed back into Ohio around 1750. The Shawnee supported the French in their long war against the British, then supported the British against the Americans during the Revolutionary War. Eventually, the Shawnee—pressured by both whites and Iroquois—lost all their lands in the east and were settled on reservations in Oklahoma.

Most modern historians believe that the reports about Henry Hamilton (1734?-1795) buying scalps are more fiction than fact.

Indiana before George Rogers Clark

The earliest inhabitants of Indiana were the same nomadic Paleo-Indians who first inhabited the other Midwest states. About 6,000 years ago, the large game that these Paleo-Indians hunted disappeared. The Native Americans survived by hunting small animals, fishing, and gathering edible plants. This culture, known as the Archaic, lasted in Indiana until about 500 B.C. It was eventually replaced by people known as the mound builders because of the huge earth mounds they built. The mounds were used mainly for burial sites, but they also served as foundations for temples and fortresses. Such mounds are found throughout Indiana, although most are in the southern part of the state.

The mound-builder culture is divided into three distinct groups. Adena, the earliest, was centered in the Ohio River valley about 2,500 years ago. The Hopewell people followed, building larger and more elaborate mounds. They also traded extensively; their mounds have yielded obsidian from the Black Hills in South Dakota, copper from the upper Great Lakes, silver from Canada, shells from both coasts, and alligator teeth from Florida. About A.D. 700, the Mississippian culture appeared. At Angel Site, a dig near Evansville, Indiana, archaeologists have uncovered the remains of a walled village of about 1,500 people that was apparently a political or religious capital of the Mississippian culture in the area.

Around 1100, people of the Algonquian language group began moving into Indiana from the north and west, including the Delaware, Miami, Potawatomi, and Shawnee.

Even as these Indians moved into Indiana, their lives were about to change due to the presence of Europeans in what had long been a virtually empty frontier. In 1679, René Robert Cavelier, sieur de La Salle, became the first European to visit the region as he made his way south from Canada and down the Mississippi River.

La Salle was followed by other French explorers and by fur traders and trappers who soon won the the friendship of the local peoples. By about 1720, the French had built forts near present-day Fort Wayne and Lafayette. These two forts and a stronghold established at Vincennes became links in a chain of forts built to prevent British fur traders from extending their trade into territory claimed by the French. Vincennes was the first permanent settlement of the French in Indiana. Historians believe settlers were there before 1727, and a fort was built in about 1732.

In late 1777, Clark went to Virginia to convince Governor Henry to back him in his plans to attack the British. According to Clark, Henry approved his plan but advised secrecy to keep the Indians and British from discovering his strategy. Consequently, Henry gave Clark open orders to protect Kentucky from attack by Indians, along with a secret letter that ordered him to attack Kaskaskia and other forts in what was then known as the Illinois Country. At the same time, Henry promoted Clark to lieutenant colonel, granted him money for supplies, and gave him a commission to raise a force of 350 men.

From Virginia, Clark made his way to Fort Pitt, where he picked up supplies. He then raised a force of about 170 men. Worried that his men might desert if they knew the full scope of his plans, he did not immediately tell his recruits where they were bound. In May 1778, he and his men—along with a number of settlers who hoped to claim land in Kentucky—set out in flatboats on the Ohio River. On May 27, the group arrived at the "Falls of the Ohio," a spot where the water was white with rapids. There Clark spied a small island in the middle of the falls, and he instructed his men to set up camp there. The city of Louisville, Kentucky, would grow opposite this island, on the south bank of the river.

On June 24, after establishing this tiny settlement, Clark and his companions continued their journey down the Ohio River in their flatboats. They left behind a few men who had become ill and the families that had accompanied Clark's army on its

In his memoirs, Clark wrote about setting up camp on the island at the Falls of the Ohio. "I observed that the little island of about seven acres . . . was seldom or never entirely covered by the water. I resolved to take possession and fortify it, . . . dividing the island among the families that had followed me for gardens. These families I now found to be a real asset, as they occasioned but little expense and with the invalids would hold this little post until we should be able to occupy the mainland. . . . "

Located just above the falls, Corn Island has since been washed away by the Ohio River.

voyage down the Ohio. Poling their flatboats into the center of the river, they shot the rapids during a total eclipse of the sun, which caused, Clark said, "various conjectures among the superstitious."

Clark knew that if he and his small army made their way into the Illinois Country by river, they would almost certainly be discovered. He ordered the flatboats abandoned at the mouth of the Tennessee River, and then he and his riflemen set out on foot. Traveling single file with little baggage, in what Clark described as "the Indian mode," they marched northwest 125 miles across the wilderness of southern Illinois in six days.

By the evening of July 4, Clark and his men were just a few miles from Kaskaskia. Questioning a family he found living in a cabin near the fort, he learned those inside were unprepared for an attack. "I was now convinced that it was impossible that the inhabitants could make any resistance," he later wrote. "My object now was to conduct matters so as to get possession of the place with as little confusion as possible, but to have it even at the loss of the whole town."

As it turned out, Kaskaskia fell without a shot being fired. At a prearranged signal, Clark and his men entered the town. Most of the residents were French, so Clark had his men who spoke French run through the streets, proclaiming that the town was captured and warning that anyone who appeared outside would be shot. Within two hours, the town was secured, its commandant captured, and its inhabitants disarmed.

Just before Clark's party left the river to travel on foot, they spotted a solitary canoe behind them. It was William Linn, one of the settlers left behind on Corn Island. When a letter from Fort Pitt had arrived shortly after Clark left the island, Linn volunteered to bring the news to Clark. The news was good and well timed: France had become America's ally! Rather than make the dangerous trip back alone, Linn joined Clark's army. Out of respect and gratitude for his bravery, Clark made Linn a major.

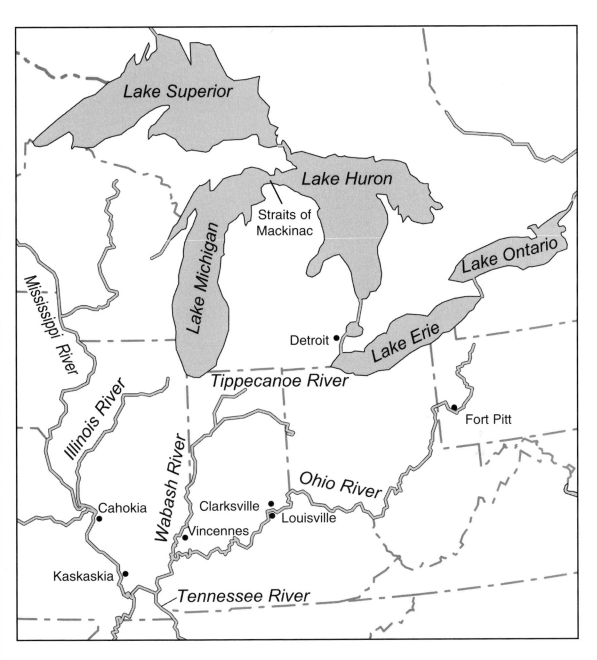

Clark and his men journeyed by river for much of the distance from Fort Pitt to their objectives—Kaskaskia and Vincennes.

Clark quickly won over the residents of the town when he told them he had come as a friend, not an enemy, and that France had recently joined the Americans in their struggle against Great Britain. Clark then promised to respect them and their property. In short order, Clark sent emissaries, including Father Pierre Gibault, to other settlements in the region. The French in these settlements knew and trusted Gibault, and they also accepted Clark's terms without any resistance.

Clark negotiates with the residents of Kaskaskia, including Father Pierre Gibault (center), who then acted as Clark's spokesman.

One of the settlements Clark captured in this bloodless conflict was Vincennes, an important post on the Wabash River. Learning from French traders at Kaskaskia that Vincennes and its post, Fort Sackville, were unprotected, Clark dispatched one of his aides, Captain Leonard Helm, with a platoon to hold Vincennes. With the occupation of Vincennes in August 1778, Clark—without a firing a shot—had eliminated British power south of Detroit.

Next, Clark turned his attention to the dozen or so Native American tribes that lived in the region. For five weeks, he met with the tribes in Cahokia, Illinois. Clark insisted that the Americans wanted only peace, that the Americans and French were now friends, and he persuaded them to stop helping the British.

Meanwhile, Governor Henry Hamilton was not about to let Clark simply capture these important outposts without a fight. Upon learning of the occupation of the forts, Hamilton gathered a force of regular British soldiers, French volunteers, and Indian allies and traveled down the Maumee and Wabash Rivers from Detroit, forcing Helm to surrender Fort Sackville in mid-December.

Then Hamilton made a huge tactical blunder. Instead of immediately attacking Clark and his small force, now back at Kaskaskia, Hamilton decided to wait until spring. Convinced Clark and his men would not leave the comfort of Kaskaskia until the weather turned warm, he sent his regular troops back to Detroit and told his Indian forces to return to their homes until the snows melted.

At Cahokia, Clark explained the Revolutionary War to the tribes gathered in this way: "A great many years ago, our forefathers lived in England, but the King oppressed them. . . . They were obliged to cross the great waters. We grew to be a great people. The King [made] us pay tribute. We bore their taxes for many years. . . . By such usage we got poor . . . and at last we complained. The King got mad and made his soldiers kill some of our people. The old men then held a great council [the Continental Congress] and made the Tomahawk very sharp [declared war] and put it into the hands of the young men, told them to be strong and strike the English."

George Rogers Clark spoke to the Native Americans at Cahokia. He asked them to "set still and look on" rather than continue to help the British.

When, in late January 1779, Clark learned of the fall of Vincennes and Hamilton's dismissal of his troops, he immediately sprang into action. Within five days, he recruited French militia to strengthen his small band of Kentuckians and set out across Illinois from Kaskaskia with a force of about 170 men. Clark was convinced he would be able to surprise Hamilton's forces and recapture Fort Sackville at Vincennes. "[T]he enemy," he later wrote, "could not suppose that we should be so mad as to attempt to march 80 leagues [about 250 miles] through a drowned country in the depths of winter."

The terrain Clark and his men had to cross was an untamed wilderness of thick woodlands punctuated by prairies and marshy wetlands. Heavy winter rains had turned marshes into lakes and creeks and rivers into raging torrents, making the journey almost impossible. There was not even a trail for the small army to follow, since traffic into the frontier normally went by river. "It was difficult and very fatiguing marching," Clark said.

When Clark and his men neared Vincennes, they discovered that the rain-swollen Wabash had surrounded the outpost like a giant natural moat. The sight of the inland sea that surrounded their target, Clark later wrote, "would have been enough to have stopped any set of men that was not in the same temper we was."

But George Rogers Clark was not about to be stopped. Instead, he ordered his men to press on. "Our suffering for four days in crossing those waters, and the manner it was done . . . is too incredible for any person to believe," he later wrote. The men struggled hour after hour in near-freezing water that reached up to their waists, holding heavy muskets over their heads to keep them dry. Sleet and icy rain fell in sheets. The men slept without fires on patches of damp ground in soaked clothing. They ran out of food. Finally, on February 23, the men reached high ground about a mile from the fort.

An illustration of Clark's daring "Expedition across the Drowned Lands"

By that time, some of Clark's men were too tired even to drag themselves from the water. These men had to be helped ashore by their stronger friends and dragged to small fires where the soldiers huddled as they tried to get warm and dry. As they slowly dried out, they spied several men on horseback, hunting for water birds. They captured one of the hunters, who told Clark that the British garrison in Fort Sackville, under the command of Henry Hamilton, consisted of a few hundred men.

Clark decided to write a letter to the inhabitants of Vincennes, telling them he was ready to attack and urging them to stay inside their homes if they were friends of the Americans. At sundown on February 25, he sent his prisoner to the town with the letter. He and his men followed close behind and deployed themselves in a way that made it appear their number was much larger than it actually was.

At a signal from Clark, the attack began. Clark, with the main body of his men, quickly took possession of the town while another group of about 14 frontiersmen began firing at the fort itself. The attack took the British in the fort so unaware that they first thought the shots were fired by residents in the town. With the town taken, Clark and the balance of his men surrounded the fort, firing through open peepholes with deadly accuracy as they turned Sackville into a walled prison for the British soldiers inside. All night the firing continued. In the morning, Clark and Hamilton began negotiating the fort's surrender. After several hours, Hamilton reluctantly gave up the fight and turned his men and the fort over to Clark.

Clark's recapture of this important outpost was one of the major American victories during the war. Historian Page Smith called Clark's campaign against the British "the most brilliant single military accomplishment of the Revolution." Though it was—compared to most battles—little more than a skirmish, it put the Midwest firmly in American hands and opened the door for a flood of immigrants down the Ohio River.

Perhaps most important, the American presence in Vincennes and Kaskaskia made it possible for Benjamin Franklin—during peace negotiations at the end of the war—to press American claims for territories that stretched west from the colonies all the way to the Mississippi River and north as far as the Great Lakes.

Sadly for Clark, his campaign against Vincennes proved to be the high point of his life. Though he fought other battles against the British and the Indians, he was, by the end of the war, in financial trouble because of his public service. To pay for his campaigns, he had spent his own money and borrowed heavily, counting on promises that he would eventually be repaid. Vouchers for his expenses were lost, however, and Clark was never repaid. Eventually, his indebtedness forced him to give up his land in Kentucky.

Clark later surveyed the area along the Ohio River, and then in 1803, he retired to a small plot of land near Clarksville, Indiana, a town he had founded in 1784. There he built a two-room cabin on a beautiful point of land overlooking the Falls of the Ohio, the same falls he had navigated with his men on their way to capture Kaskaskia in 1779.

In 1809, doctors were forced to amputate Clark's right leg. He had suffered a stroke that paralyzed his right side, and some historians believe this made the amputation necessary. Another story maintains his leg was badly burned when he fell into his fireplace and that the wound would not heal. (The fall was perhaps caused by the effects of the

92

General William H. Harrison (1773-1841) at the Battle of Tippecanoe. He also led U.S. forces at the Battle of the Thames, fought in Ontario in 1813, during which Tecumseh was killed. Harrison was elected president of the U.S., but died after only one month in office.

known as the Prophet, led a spiritual revival, preaching a return to traditional Indian ways and religion. On November 6, 1811, after a failed attempt to reach a peace accord, Harrison marched a force of about 900 men to within three miles of Tippecanoe, the village created by the two Shawnee brothers. In charge while Tecumseh traveled south to gather more support, Tenskwatawa ordered a night attack. Harrison's men held off the Native American warriors, and the next day burned their abandoned village, giving the conflict its name: the Battle of Tippecanoe.

Though Tecumseh's confederacy was broken by this defeat, Native Americans in Indiana continued to resist white settlement. Many raided settlers and fought with the British against the United States in the War of 1812.

In December 1815, after the United States and Britain signed the Treaty of Ghent ending the War of 1812, the Indiana territorial legislature drew up a petition for statehood. The petition was approved by Congress and a state constitution was written. On December 1, 1816, Indiana became the 19th state to enter the Union.

stroke.) Whatever the cause, this surgery was performed without any anesthetic, as—at Clark's request—two fifers and two drummers played outside the window of the operating room for two hours while doctors removed the war hero's leg. Unable to live alone following this surgery, Clark moved to Locust Grove, not far from Louisville, Kentucky, across the Ohio River from Clarksville. There he lived with his sister, Lucy, and her husband.

In the fall of 1812, when news of Clark's crippled condition spread, the government of Virginia voted to award the old soldier a commemorative sword and an annual pension of $400. Six years later, George Rogers Clark suffered another stroke and died on February 13, 1818.

Indiana from Clark to Statehood

When the Revolutionary War came to an end, Indiana and the area we know as the Midwest was claimed by Virginia and several other states. Not long after the end of the war, these states ceded their claims to the federal government. In 1787, the Northwest Ordinance became law, organizing the possessions north of the Ohio River as the Northwest Territory and opening them to settlement.

Land-hungry settlers poured into the new territory from the East. The Native Americans who lived in the region became alarmed and angry. In 1790, President George Washington ordered troops to subdue the Indians. Little Turtle, a Miami chief, cleverly routed the first two American forces sent to Ohio and Indiana, but Native American resistance ended in August 1794, when General Anthony Wayne and his soldiers crushed the Indian forces at the Battle of Fallen Timbers, near present-day Toledo, Ohio. One year later, Little Turtle and 1,100 other chiefs and warriors ceded all of Ohio and most of Indiana.

In 1800, the U.S. Congress carved the Indiana Territory out of the western part of

the Northwest Territory. At the time, this huge area, which included almost all of what is now Indiana—as well as Michigan, Wisconsin, Illinois, and part of Minnesota— had only about 5,000 residents. William Henry Harrison, who later became president of the United States, was appointed first governor of the Indiana Territory. Vincennes was designated the capital.

During the first decade of the 1800s, Indiana's population grew to more than 24,000. At the same time, the territory was greatly reduced in size as large areas of land were carved off to form the Michigan Territory (1805) and Illinois Territory

(1809). During these years, Harrison convinced Native American groups living in the territory to cede their land to the government. Many of these tribes later regretted making the agreements because they received very little for their lands.

Angry at what they viewed as unfair treatment at the hands of the government, several Indian groups banded together under the leadership of Shawnee chief Tecumseh. Tecumseh wanted a separate Indian nation in the Great Lakes and Ohio River valley region and realized a unified action among all the tribes was needed for this to happen. His brother, Tenskwatawa,

Later a general for the British during the War of 1812, Tecumseh (1768-1813) was responsible for many of the early British successes, including the fall of Detroit.

Shawnee mystic Tenskwatawa (1768-1837) was the twin brother of Tecumseh. He preached a return to traditional Indian ways.

General William H. Harrison (1773-1841) at the Battle of Tippecanoe. He also led U.S. forces at the Battle of the Thames, fought in Ontario in 1813, during which Tecumseh was killed. Harrison was elected president of the U.S., but died after only one month in office.

known as the Prophet, led a spiritual revival, preaching a return to traditional Indian ways and religion. On November 6, 1811, after a failed attempt to reach a peace accord, Harrison marched a force of about 900 men to within three miles of Tippecanoe, the village created by the two Shawnee brothers. In charge while Tecumseh traveled south to gather more support, Tenskwatawa ordered a night attack. Harrison's men held off the Native American warriors, and the next day burned their abandoned village, giving the conflict its name: the Battle of Tippecanoe.

Though Tecumseh's confederacy was broken by this defeat, Native Americans in Indiana continued to resist white settlement. Many raided settlers and fought with the British against the United States in the War of 1812.

In December 1815, after the United States and Britain signed the Treaty of Ghent ending the War of 1812, the Indiana territorial legislature drew up a petition for statehood. The petition was approved by Congress and a state constitution was written. On December 1, 1816, Indiana became the 19th state to enter the Union.

Chapter Five

Rufus Putnam
and the
Pioneers of Ohio

On December 3, 1787, a group of covered wagons began a journey from Ipswich, Massachusetts. The wagons, carrying 47 men, were bound for what was then considered the western frontier. Each one was painted with a sign that read, "For the Ohio." The leader of this group of pioneer settlers, many of whom were veterans of the Revolutionary War, was General Rufus Putnam, himself a war veteran and a protégé of President George Washington.

Rufus Putnam was born on April 9, 1738, in Sutton, Massachusetts, a half-century before that wagon train of people set out to found the first settlement in what would become the state of Ohio. He was the son of Elisha Putnam and his wife, Susanna, and the direct descendent of John Putnam,

Soldier and surveyor Rufus Putnam (1738-1824) convinced the fledgling nation to make land in Ohio available to Revolutionary War veterans.

one of the earliest settlers of the Massachusetts Bay Colony.

We know little of Rufus Putnam's early life other than the facts that his father died when Rufus was a boy of seven and that his mother soon married John Sadler, an innkeeper. Following his mother's second marriage, Rufus was sent to live with a succession of relatives until he was apprenticed to a millwright at the age of 16. (A millwright is someone who makes or fixes the machinery that mills, or grinds, grain.) Rufus must have been a bright young man, for he educated himself. Though he studied geography and history, he concentrated most of his energy on the study of mathematics.

In the years from 1754 to 1763, while Rufus was a young man in Massachusetts, the British and French were engaged in the French and Indian War, waged to determine who would have control of North America and all its riches. This war was the last in a long series of conflicts that had started in the late 1600s. By the mid-1700s, the British were determined to end the French presence in North America. Many colonists, themselves tired of threats from the French and their Indian allies, joined to help the British drive the French from the disputed lands.

In 1757, Putnam enlisted in the army. His knowledge of mathematics served him well as a soldier. He constructed a series of defensive works in the Lake Champlain region and won a promotion to the rank of sergeant in 1759, when he was just 21 years of age.

In December 1760, Putnam returned to New Braintree, Massachusetts. He married a young woman named Elizabeth Ayers on April 6, 1761. In November of the following year, Elizabeth died, almost certainly in childbirth since she left an infant son who died about a year later. On January 10, 1765, Putnam was married for the second time, to Persis Rice. Their marriage lasted 55 years, until Persis died in 1820. During those years, the couple had nine children.

In the 1760s and early 1770s, Putnam worked his farm outside New Braintree, built mills using skills he had learned as an apprentice, and taught himself surveying. In 1773, he was part of a group sent to explore and survey lands in the lower Mississippi River valley. (Surveying measures the area and elevation of a piece of land using angles on the earth's surface. Land is often surveyed to set boundaries or lay out construction.) These lands were being claimed as bounties for veterans of the French and Indian War. While this project ultimately failed, it interested Putnam in the idea of colonizing western lands and, just as important, made him a supporter of using land as a reward for military service.

Putnam's life changed direction sharply with the start of the Revolutionary War. Turning his back on farming and constructing mills, he enlisted in the Continental Army in 1775, in the earliest days of the conflict. Recognizing Putnam's value as an engineer, the army granted him a commission as a lieutenant colonel.

We get a good idea about Putnam's personality from a verse he carved on his powder horn (an animal's horn capped at one end, used to store gunpowder): "Amour [love] of words and not of deeds
Is like a garden full of weeds."

Rufus Putnam was a true hero of the Revolutionary War. He fought in the battle for Breed's Hill, overlooking Boston, Massachusetts, known today as the Battle of Bunker Hill (pictured here). He helped plan the attack on Stony Point in New York. In addition, he designed fortifications at West Point, the site of the United States Military Academy.

In the winter of 1775-1776, Putnam was placed in charge of building defensive works around the city of Boston, then in the hands of the British. After building wooden defenses that made it impossible for the British to capture the high ground outside the city, he was sent to build defensive works near New York City. Putnam was so successful that, in August 1776, Congress appointed him a full colonel—just one step below a general—and made him the army's chief engineer. Putnam, however, wanted Congress to organize a corps of engineers as a separate part of the army. When the lawmakers took no action, Putnam resigned his commission.

Unwilling to stand on the sidelines during the war between the colonies and Britain, Putnam accepted the command of a Massachusetts regiment. He was in several battles during the war and ultimately achieved the rank of brigadier general.

During the war years, Putnam became friendly with another general, George Washington. He also became a spokesman for officers and soldiers who often went long periods without any pay for their service and who—after the Revolutionary War ended in 1783—were treated with what many viewed as disdain by the new government of the United States.

In June 1783, as a spokesman for disenchanted military men, Rufus Putnam framed the Newburgh Petition. This document, signed by 288 veteran officers, asked the government to give veterans so-called bounty lands in what was then known as the Ohio Country. Washington, by then the first president of the United States, supported the petition. Congress, however, had not yet passed any laws providing land for former soldiers and officers, so the petition died.

Following this failure, Putnam went to Maine to survey land then owned by Massachusetts. He was there in 1785 when Thomas Hutchins, geographer of the United States, chose him to be deputy surveyor of the land north of the Ohio River, east of the Mississippi River, and south of the Great Lakes that had been ceded to the United States by Britain after the Revolutionary War. Busy in Maine, Putnam delegated Ben Tupper, a young surveyor

Ohio before Putnam

Long before the first European set foot in what we know as Ohio, the region was inhabited by the mound builders, members of a group that constructed earthen mounds in a large area from the Great Lakes to the Gulf of Mexico and from the Mississippi River to the Appalachian Mountains. Over centuries, these prehistoric people were replaced by a later mound-builder culture called the Mississippian. Living in stockaded villages, these early inhabitants of Ohio survived by hunting with bows and arrows and growing large quantities of corn, beans, and squash.

The Eries, a Woodland tribe that had followed the mound builders, were driven from Ohio in the late 1650s by the powerful Iroquois, who conquered many other

Some Woodland tribes built lodges such as these.

peoples from the Atlantic Ocean to the Mississippi River in wars over the fur trade.

By the late 1690s, Native Americans from other areas began migrating to Ohio. Some came in search of game or land for farming, while others came in an attempt to escape white settlers who were moving ever westward. Among the Indian people who moved to Ohio were the Huron and Ottawa from the north and a band of Iroquois called Mingo. The Delaware and Shawnee moved to Ohio from the east, while the Miami moved from the west.

As the French and British fought for control of the rich fur lands that included Ohio during the French and Indian War, the Native Americans were, for the most part, allies of the French. At the end of that war in 1763, Great Britain emerged victorious and France gave up most of its lands in the north, including all of the Ohio country.

Unhappy at the prospect of being ruled by the British, Ottawa chief Pontiac led a rebellion. At first, this Indian revolt was successful, as Pontiac's forces captured most of the British forts in the vast region north and west of the Ohio River. After learning they would not get help from the French, however, Pontiac signed a treaty ending the war. The native groups of Ohio later sided with the British during the American Revolution, and again were disappointed. After losing that war, the British ceded the territory to the United States, allowing a new group of settlers to encroach upon Indian land.

who was engaged to be married to Putnam's daughter Martha, to conduct the survey for him.

That fall, after traveling to the west on Putnam's behalf, Tupper returned to report to Putnam about the western lands. The two men decided to form a company to buy land in Ohio for Revolutionary War veterans. Their plan called for the company—known as the Ohio Company—to issue 1,000 shares worth $1,000 each. These shares could be bought by Revolutionary War veterans using depreciated continental "certificates of debt."

With this capital, plus $10 per share in gold paid by veterans, the company would buy acreage in the Ohio lands and then assign parcels to its war veteran investors.

To promote their idea, Rufus Putnam and Ben Tupper organized meetings of veterans at taverns throughout Massachusetts. They took out advertisements in newspapers seeking veterans who wished to settle in what the promoters described as "that delightful region," Ohio. The Ohio Company sent Manasseh Cutler to New York as a lobbyist. Cutler, an ordained Congregational minister as well as a physician and a lawyer, skillfully negotiated with Congress. The contract ultimately signed by company officials, including Cutler, called for the United States government to sell the Ohio Company the land it wanted for $1 an acre, discounted to 66¢ per acre. Since the land was to be paid for in U.S. certificates of debt, however, the real cost was only about 7¢ per acre.

The multitalented Manasseh Cutler (1742-1823) also served in the U.S. House of Representatives from 1801 to 1805.

While this bargaining was going on, Congress was struggling to determine the type of government to be established in what was already known as the Northwest Territory. In July 1787, the Ordinance of 1787, also known as the Northwest Ordinance, was passed. Among other things, this legislation allowed Congress to appoint a governor, forbade slavery, made freedom of religion mandatory, and said that any territory within the region could petition for statehood once its population reached 60,000 persons.

In the months following the signing of the contract between the Ohio Company and Congress, preparations were made for a group of settlers to head west from Massachusetts to the company's lands on the north bank of the Ohio River. On December 3, 1787, this group of settlers, made up of 47 men, left Ipswich, Massachusetts. By that time, the company had named Rufus Putnam the "Superintendent of all the business relating to the settlement of their lands in the Territory North-west of the Ohio." Putnam joined his group on their journey west in Hartford, Connecticut, on January 1, 1788.

Most of the men in the first wave of settlers were shareholders in the Ohio Company. These men, according to a contemporary report, "wisely desired to see the country before removing their families into a region so far in advance of population." According to Manasseh Cutler, more than 150 men applied to go with this first wave of would-be settlers. "They have almost refused to [accept] a denial," Cutler wrote. "The men I have engaged are equal to any I would have chosen." Included in this number were three carpenters, two blacksmiths, and a number of farmers—just the kind of men needed to establish a new settlement on the frontier.

Leaving Ipswich, the covered wagons made their way across the Allegheny Mountains. The winter of 1787-1788 was, in the words of one historian, a season "of uncommon severity." The mountains the party had to cross were so deep in snow that the men had to abandon their wagons and construct sledges to drag their tools and belongings over the mountains.

The Land and the Northwest Ordinances

The Northwest Territory was the name given to a vast area of land that included what are now the states of Ohio, Indiana, Illinois, Michigan, Wisconsin, and the eastern part of Minnesota. This area, totaling almost 250,000 square miles, was ceded by Britain to the United States in 1783, at the end of the Revolutionary War. What to do with the land became an immediate problem for the young government of the United States. On the basis of their early colonial charters, 7 of the 13 states claimed most of this land. The other states refused to recognize these claims and insisted that the territory should belong to the country as a whole. It took almost 20 years, but one by one the seven states yielded their claims.

While ownership questions were being resolved, the U.S. Congress passed the Land Ordinance on May 20, 1785. This document established the basic unit of land, a township. A township was 36 square miles; each square mile equaled 640 acres and was called a section. A section was the smallest piece of land a settler could purchase. (This was later changed so people could purchase half sections, 320 acres, or even quarter sections of 160 acres.) Land would be auctioned off, first come, first served, with Congress acting as a real-estate agent.

Settlers listen to the terms of the Northwest Ordinance.

"With this one decision on the division of land into townships and sections, they determined what kind of country America would be," wrote historian Ted Morgan. "It would not be like Europe, where only kings, the nobility, and the church could own land. It would be a country where *anybody* could own land, a pie with millions of slices."

Now that Congress had determined how the land would be divided, the Northwest Territory needed a plan of government. The Northwest Ordinance was passed in 1787 and provided for the formation of between three and five territories that could eventually become states. Congress was given the power to appoint a governor, secretary, and three judges to oversee a territory. The ordinance allowed a territory to set up its own legislature and send a nonvoting representative to Congress once the population reached 5,000 voters. A territory could ask to become a state when its population reached 60,000 inhabitants. Religious freedom was guaranteed and slavery outlawed.

The article of the ordinance banning slavery was the work of Nathan Dane, a U.S. representative from Massachusetts. The article was in his handwriting on a separate piece of paper that was attached to the ordinance at the last minute. Dane later wrote that when it was read it was approved unanimously, "to the great honor of the slave-holding states."

In October 1787, General Arthur St. Clair, a Revolutionary War hero, was appointed the first governor of the Northwest Territory. In July 1800, the western part of the territory was constituted into the Indiana Territory; Michigan and Illinois Territories were created out of Indiana Territory in 1805 and 1809, respectively; and in April 1836, part of Michigan Territory was organized into the territory of Wisconsin.

Nathan Dane (1752-1835)

Finally, in mid-February, Putnam and his followers reached the Youghiogheny River in southwest Pennsylvania, about 20 miles south of Pittsburgh. For the next six weeks, the tired men recovered from the difficult midwinter mountain crossing. During this time, they built a small flotilla of flatboats to carry them and their belongings. They traveled north on the Youghiogheny to the Monongahela River, which flows into the Ohio River, and then down the Ohio to the Muskingum River in eastern Ohio. On April 7, the party reached the mouth of the Muskingum.

It took four months for Rufus Putnam and the other settlers to reach their new home in southeast Ohio.

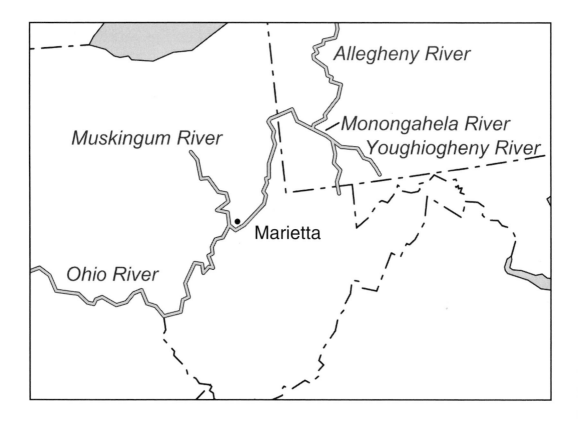

Immediately, they began clearing the land and laying out lots. Within five days, they had cleared five acres in a small triangle between the Ohio and Muskingum Rivers. A week later, enough land had been cleared to allow the directors to parcel out lots. The settlers named their new home Marietta after Marie Antoinette, who had been the queen of France, an American ally, during the American Revolution.

Putnam and the other settlers were amazed by the nature all around them. They saw a black walnut tree 22 feet in circumference, clams as big as dinner plates, and huge catfish. After planting corn in their newly cleared fields, they claimed they were stunned to watch it grow several inches in a day.

In its earliest days, the first permanent settlement in Ohio was much like a military camp. A stockade, called Campus Martius, was built with blockhouses at each corner and a high palisade protecting rows of tents, and later houses, in which company shareholders lived.

During these early days, Rufus Putnam—whose dream it had been to reward Revolutionary War veterans with cheap lands in the West—was Marietta's "superintendent" or top officer. Self-educated, he was one of the founders and trustees of a school that became Marietta College. He also put his wartime experience to good use, advising the settlers on how to protect themselves against attacks by Native Americans.

At first, these steps to guard against Indian attack might have seemed foolish to some of the

Settlers used flatboats like this one to transport goods down the Ohio River. The boats had no oars or sails; they simply flowed with the current while people steered with tillers.

An engraving of Campus Martius, Marietta, Ohio, made in 1791.

settlers. In the months immediately following the establishment of Marietta, the settlers maintained an uneasy peace with the Indians. By late 1790, however, that situation changed. The Indians living near the settlement—including the Wyandot, Delaware, Ottawa, Ojibwa, Potawatomi, and Sauk— grew angry that white settlers were taking over their land. Skirmishes between the Native Americans and settlers became commonplace. Marietta itself was attacked and an outlying settlement at Big Bottom, about 30 miles northwest of the first settlement, was destroyed and 12 men were killed.

During this period, in March 1790, Putnam was named a judge of the Northwest Territory. Two years later, he was made a brigadier general in the regular U.S. Army, with instructions to deal with the Indians who lived in the area. In this capacity, he negotiated a peace treaty. Unfortunately, the treaty negotiated by Putnam did not stop the fighting in the Ohio Territory. It was not until late 1794, following the defeat of the Ohio tribes by General Anthony Wayne, that peace came to Marietta and the other frontier settlements in Ohio.

Impulsive and quick-tempered, General Anthony Wayne (1745-1796) was sometimes referred to as "Mad Anthony." He was an able general, however, winning several important victories for the colonies during the Revolutionary War.

The Ohio River viewed at Marietta during the 1870s

Historian Ted Morgan called the surveyor "a neglected figure in the saga of the west." Putnam and others who mapped the new lands for purchase faced the same hardships and dangers as explorers and mountain men, but received little recognition.

Meanwhile, as Marietta slowly grew from a frontier outpost to a thriving town, the Ohio Company, strapped by debt, ceased to exist. In 1796, freed from his job as director of the company, Rufus Putnam was appointed surveyor general of the United States. From 1797 to 1803, he surveyed unmapped parts of Ohio. In 1802, he was named a delegate to the Ohio constitutional convention. In that role, he exerted a strong influence to keep slavery out of the territory.

Following that public service, Putnam—who had risen to power largely due to the patronage of

George Washington—fell out of favor with those in office. In his sixties, he began spending more time with his family, became a devout churchgoer, and wrote his memoirs. In 1804, he became one of the founders of Ohio University in Athens. Rufus Putnam, who had used his talents and desire for success to become a Revolutionary War hero and one of the most influential men in the Northwest Territory, died in Marietta on May 4, 1824, at the age of 86.

His memory, as well as some of the original Campus Martius buildings, have been preserved at a state memorial. In 2003, Marietta College continued to educate young people, and the town of Marietta, with a population of 14,500, remained a small commercial center for the flourishing farms around it.

In 1807, a visitor from New York to Marietta described the town as "New England in miniature." The settlers, he added, "are sober, honest, religious, and industrious, while dissipation and irrational amusements are not known in friendly circles."

This photograph of Rufus Putnam's house in Marietta was taken in 1895. Some of the original buildings are preserved at the Campus Martius State Memorial.

Ohio from Settlement to Statehood

Shortly after Rufus Putnam and his group established Marietta, several other settlements were started, including Losantiville, located opposite the mouth of Kentucky's Licking River. In 1790 General Arthur St. Clair, a Revolutionary War hero who had been named the first governor of the Northwest Territory, made his headquarters at Losantiville and changed the settlement's name to Cincinnati.

For a time, Native Americans in Ohio resisted the influx of settlers into the lands they had long considered theirs. These attempts ended after August 1794, however, when General Anthony Wayne defeated the Native Americans at the Battle of Fallen Timbers, near present-day Maumee. The end of the conflict between the settlers and Indians led to another wave of migration into the region.

By December 1798, the number of free adult males in the Northwest Territory had reached 5,000. This was the number required by the Northwest Ordinance of 1787 for election of a territorial legislature. The new Territorial House of Representatives assembled in Cincinnati in 1799 and chose as its president Edward Tiffin, a 31-year-old Virginian who had arrived in the territory just two years earlier. Another former Virginian, William Henry Harrison, was elected territorial delegate to the Congress of the United States.

Almost as soon as Harrison arrived in Washington, D.C., he sponsored a bill to divide the Northwest Territory along a line running north from the mouth of the Kentucky River. The eastern area, encompassing roughly the land we know as the state of Ohio, remained the Northwest Territory. The western area, stretching to the Mississippi River, was named the Indiana Territory.

Arthur St. Clair (1734-1818) was a controversial governor whom Thomas Jefferson removed from office in 1802 because St. Clair opposed statehood for Ohio.

The population of the newly defined Northwest Territory grew quickly to almost 60,000. Under an act signed by President Thomas Jefferson, delegates were elected to draw up a constitution for the proposed new state of Ohio, whose western boundary was redrawn as a line running due north from where the Ohio and Great Miami Rivers meet. On March 1, 1803, Ohio became the nation's 17th state.

The Miami, led by Little Turtle, defeated the forces of General Arthur St. Clair in 1792. The Indians were decisively beaten two years later, however, by General Anthony Wayne (center).

COPYRIGHT-1907
by C.L.TRUDELL

Chapter Six

Julien Dubuque
and the
First Settlement in Iowa

Julien Dubuque, famous today as one of the first permanent European settlers in Iowa, was born on January 10, 1762, in the Trois-Rivières area of Quebec to Noel Augustin Dubuque and his wife, Marie. Julien was the youngest of their 13 children.

Noel Dubuque was a farmer. Like most farmers' sons, Julien probably spent much of his childhood working in the fields, tending livestock, and performing chores around the family's home. Growing up on the frontier, he probably also learned to hunt, trap, and fish.

At the age of six or seven, Julien started school. His education began at the Roman Catholic parish school in his village and continued later in a secondary school in the village of Sorel, not far from his home. His actions in later life—particularly his

This likeness of Julien Dubuque (1762-1810) was made from descriptions of the man; no portraits of him exist.

Sorel is located about 40 miles northeast of Montreal, where the Richelieu and St. Lawrence Rivers meet. The town was named for Pierre de Saurel, the commander of the first French fort built on the site in 1642.

When Julien Dubuque came to Prairie du Chien in 1782, the French had been trading there at a post on the eastern banks of the Mississippi River since 1673. A fort was erected in 1685. Prairie du Chien (Prairie of the Dog) is the second oldest settlement in Wisconsin. The city was named in honor of a local Native American chief.

ability to express himself well both in speech and in writing—gives evidence that he must have been a good student.

Sometime in the early 1780s, when Julien was a young man of 18 or 19 years of age, his father died. Julien then left home to find his fortune in the vast territory that had been named "Louisiana" by René La Salle more than a century before Julien's birth. When Julien set off for Louisiana, the northern reaches of the Mississippi River had been fully explored by French traders and trappers. Forts and trading posts were scattered throughout the region. Dubuque made his way to one of the most famous of these, Michilimackinac, located at the northern end of Lake Michigan. There he found a job as a clerk in a trading post.

It was probably there that Julien Dubuque, the farmer's son, learned to be an expert trader. Indeed, those skills proved to be the way he earned both his living in the wilderness and his lasting fame. Michilimackinac, however, was Dubuque's home for only a brief period. His desire for fortune and adventure soon led him to Prairie du Chien, Wisconsin, on the Mississippi River. According to Nicholas Boilvin, an Indian agent at Prairie du Chien and a friend of Dubuque, the man who would gain fame in Iowa first came to the upper Mississippi River valley in about 1782, when he was 20 years of age.

The fur trade—especially the trade for beaver pelts—was well established in the area in which Dubuque settled. He knew trading was a good way

for a hard-working young man to earn his fortune and to establish himself as a man of substance. It seems certain, too, he was looking for a special opportunity.

He found that opportunity on the western shore of the Mississippi, in an area of Iowa that was already well known to French traders as the site of a number of rich lead mines. While a few mines had

The Mississippi River bluffs near Prairie du Chien, painted by George Catlin in 1835, must have looked very similar to Dubuque when he arrived 50 years earlier.

Iowa before Dubuque

The first Iowans—like the earliest residents throughout the midwestern United States—were nomadic hunters. Some 11,000 or 12,000 years ago, these nomads entered Iowa in search of giant bison, woolly mammoth, and other large animals that moved north as glaciers that had covered large parts of North America retreated. As the climate grew warmer, some of these people remained in Iowa, where they supplemented their diet by gathering seeds, berries, and roots.

About 1,000 years ago, these early residents were replaced by people from the south who migrated north along the Mississippi River and its tributaries. These farmers, who survived by planting and harvesting corn, squash, and beans, were the forerunners of the Ioway tribe, for whom the state is named.

It was the Ioways—and members of the Illinois people—who lived in Iowa in 1673 when the French explorers Jacques Marquette and Louis Joliet became the first Europeans to visit there. These early explorers were followed, in 1681 and 1682, by the French explorer René Robert Cavelier, sieur de La Salle. Searching for the Northwest Passage, La Salle traveled down the Mississippi River to the Gulf of Mexico, claimed the entire river basin, including Iowa, for France, and named it Louisiana. While Iowa was a French territory for the next century, only a few missionaries, fur traders, and soldiers passed through the region during that period.

In 1760, near the end of the French and Indian War, the French—knowing they would lose the war and wanting to keep the lands west of the Mississippi River out of British hands—secretly transferred "ownership" of all those lands to Spain. About two decades after that, in 1788, Julien Dubuque became the first white settler in Iowa.

In the years between the time the first Europeans visited Iowa and Dubuque's day, many new Native American groups entered Iowa as they were forced west by some of the eastern tribes. These included the Omaha, Missouri, Sioux, Winnebago, Sauk, Fox, and Potawatomi. These people eventually displaced the Illinois and the Ioway peoples who were some of the region's oldest residents.

When Julien Dubuque arrived in Iowa, the Sauk and Fox were two of the strongest Native American groups living along the Mississippi River.

been established by the Sauk and Fox Indians (also called the Mesquakie) who lived in the region and controlled the output of the mines, their mining efforts were relatively small. Used to make shot for guns, lead was valuable. Dubuque wanted to mine this metal on a large scale. With an eye to gaining control of the mines, Julien Dubuque set out to win favor with the Native Americans. He learned their languages, gave them presents, and adopted some of their ways.

On September 22, 1788, the Fox Indians gave Dubuque—whom they called "Little Night" because of his short stature and dark complexion—the right to mine the area around present-day Dubuque. The Native Americans also gave him their permission to mine lands on the eastern side of the Mississippi, around present-day Galena, Illinois. The agreement read, in part: "the Foxes permit Julien Dubuque, called by them Little Night, to work at the mine as long as he shall please, . . . moreover, they sell and abandon to him, all the coast and the contents of the mine . . . so that no white man or Indian shall make any pretension to it without the consent of Sieur Julien Dubuque; and . . . he shall be free to search wherever he may think it proper to do so." This agreement between Little Night and the Foxes established Dubuque as a force to be reckoned with on the upper Mississippi River.

A popular legend said Dubuque used trickery to obtain the rights to the mine from the Fox tribe. According to one story, he threatened to burn the river if the Indians did not give him the ownership of the mines. If this legend is to be believed, Dubuque had secretly poured oil onto the river's surface. Lighting the oil on fire, he convinced the Indians he had magical powers. Astonished, the Native Americans hurriedly made him a gift of the mines.

A more likely—if less dramatic—explanation is found in the fact that the Indians seemed to genuinely like Julien Dubuque. As far as we know, he lived among the Fox for 22 years without tension or conflict. Just how fond the Indians were of Dubuque was demonstrated when Black Hawk, the famous chief of the Sauk, a tribe related to the Fox, called Dubuque "their relation." This was an affectionate term used to indicate that the French trader was more than just a friend to the Indians; he was—as far as they were concerned—a member of the family.

According to the terms of the agreement between Dubuque and the Fox, the trader could not sell the lands on which the mines were located, but he could work undisturbed and take as much lead as he could find without making any payments to the Indians. Soon after receiving permission, Dubuque started extracting lead from the mines. He also cleared land for a farm, built a furnace to smelt ore, opened a store for trade with the Indians, and constructed a home for himself and cabins for about a dozen French employees he hired to help him work the mines.

From records still in existence, we know that Dubuque's holdings, in addition to his farm and smelting furnace, included his house, a couple of storage buildings, a gristmill, and a building of some

Nicholas Boilvin described Julien Dubuque's relations with the Native Americans this way: "In the course of a few years he spent a great deal of money by his generous manner of acting, making many presents to the Indians and refusing in many instances to take their furs in exchange, contrary to the custom of the traders among them. By that means he gained the esteem and affection of the Sacs and Foxes."

Osh-e-ton-o-quot, a Fox leader, posed for this undated portrait. The Fox referred to themselves as the Meskwakihuk, or "Red-Earth People." Originally from Michigan, the Fox were driven from their homes by enemy tribes in the early seventeenth century. They resettled in Wisconsin, where they later allied themselves with the Sauk. By Dubuque's time, these Native Americans were living on both sides of the Mississippi River in Illinois and Iowa. They raised corn, beans, and squash and in the winter sent hunting parties to the west in search of buffalo.

sort near the Mississippi. His home was in the hills, a slight distance away from the river.

Though he lived in what was still the frontier, Julien Dubuque surrounded himself with fine things. Following his death, furniture, dishes, clothing, and other personal possessions were shipped from Dubuque downriver to St. Louis, where they were sold. If they were valuable enough to be packed, shipped, and resold, they were almost certainly well-made items that had been purchased either in the East or in Canada and then imported to Iowa, not the simple, homemade goods common on the frontier. The inventory made after Dubuque's death also listed 58 books. His library included a business encyclopedia, eight volumes on political science, art books, and the works of the French political philosopher Charles Louis de Secondat, baron de la Brède et de Montesquieu. This was at a time, too, when many of the most important men in America were illiterate.

The inventory of Dubuque's estate is also interesting because it includes several items of women's clothing. Personal letters sent to him refer to Madam Dubuque. While official records contain no indication that the founder of the city of Dubuque was ever married, it is likely that he took a Fox woman as his bride.

Dubuque was a man of real substance on the Mississippi River frontier within a decade of obtaining the Indians' permission to work their mines. In addition to taking lead from lodes identified by the friendly Indians who knew the region well, Dubuque also traded goods for lead brought to him by Indians. Several times each year, he shipped the lead he obtained downriver to St. Louis, Missouri, selling the ore and replenishing his stock of items to trade. He reportedly went with his goods to St. Louis, where he enjoyed the social life, sometimes playing his violin at dances.

Dubuque was a refined man who enjoyed himself in company. According to witnesses, when he visited St. Louis each year, he had a good time at the dances and balls that were an important part of the French settlers' social life. He would, one witness said, play the fiddle and dance to his own music.

In 1805, when the famous explorer Zebulon Pike came to the region, Dubuque told Pike the lead mines were producing between 20,000 and 40,000 pounds of lead per year. Based on records of how much lead was traded in the area, Dubuque underestimated the output, probably deliberately so no one would know how valuable his mines were.

Meanwhile, even though the Indians considered Dubuque a friend, and though they had treated him graciously, he was not above taking advantage of their friendship by stealing their lands. In 1796, Dubuque petitioned Francisco Luis Hector, baron de Carondelet, the governor of Louisiana (which was still controlled by Spain), to grant him full legal possession of the mines. The French pioneer made this plea despite the fact that the agreement between him and the Fox tribe clearly stated that he was granted the right to work the mines, not the outright ownership of the land.

In his petition—which asked for the possession of an area 21 miles long and almost 10 miles wide along the Mississippi—Dubuque referred to the lead mines as "the Mines of Spain," an obvious attempt to influence the Spanish governor to look favorably on his request for ownership of the land. Because this large area included land other than the lead mines, it seems reasonable to believe that Dubuque would have sold the extra land—or at least rented it—to others. That Dubuque was willing to steal land from the Indians to enrich himself makes him a less attractive figure than he would have been if he hadn't been willing to cheat his friends.

In 1805, Zebulon Montgomery Pike (1779-1813) was commissioned to take an exploration party to find the source of the Mississippi River. Although that expedition failed, in 1806 he explored what is now Colorado and New Mexico, and sighted Pikes Peak. Promoted to brigadier general during the War of 1812, he was killed in battle in 1813.

Dubuque received his grant. Before he was able to take full advantage of the lands he had been granted by Spain, the huge territory known as Louisiana was returned to France by Spain. Then in 1803, the U.S. government bought the territory from the French. Suddenly, Dubuque had to deal

The Louisiana Purchase

In 1803, President Thomas Jefferson was concerned that France, which owned the huge territory that lay west of the Mississippi River, would forbid Americans use of that waterway. Jefferson sent two representatives, James Monroe and Robert Livingston, to France to purchase Florida and New Orleans for $10 million. They came home having bought the entire Louisiana Territory, some 828,000 square miles of land between the Mississippi River and the Rocky mountains, for $15 million. The French emperor, Napoleon Bonaparte, had been in need of money to fund his wars in Europe. This acquisition roughly doubled the size of the United States, and has been called one of the greatest real-estate deals in history.

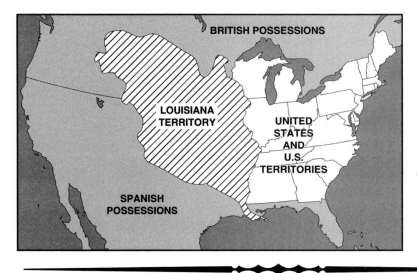

With both Great Britain and Spain neighboring the Louisiana Territory, it was important for the U.S. to begin exploring and settling this land as soon as possible.

with the U.S. government. Consequently, he filed a new claim with the Board of Land Commissioners in St. Louis. At the same time, he made a second claim for more than 7,000 acres of land on the west shore of the Mississippi, opposite Prairie du Chien.

Dubuque knew his claim to the lands around the lead mines was weak, at best. At the same time, he was badly in need of money and deeply in debt. In 1804, about a year before Pike's visit, he decided on a bold move that would both strengthen his claim and bring him some financial relief.

At that time, Auguste Chouteau, a fur trader and the founder of the city of St. Louis, was one of the most influential men in Louisiana. Having Chouteau as a supporter in his fight to obtain a free legal claim would be a great help, so Dubuque sold half the approximately 200 square miles in his claim to Chouteau for about $11,000. From that time forward, Chouteau was committed to helping Dubuque. Indeed, when the claim was filed, it was in the names of both men.

Ultimately, William Henry Harrison, governor of the Indiana Territory (and later president of the United States), ruled in favor of Dubuque and Chouteau. He did this despite the fact that he had recently signed a treaty with the Fox and Sauks, which included a provision that the U.S. government recognized the tribes' ownership of the west bank of the Mississippi River in what is now Iowa.

Even with his land grants and his expertise as a trader, Dubuque found himself deeply in debt to Chouteau, one of the richest traders in America in

Auguste Chouteau (1749-1829), Dubuque's business partner and ultimately his heir, was only 14 years old when he arrived in Missouri to make his fortune.

his time. To settle his debts, he ultimately made provisions that all his land holdings would go to the founder of St. Louis upon his death.

Death came to Dubuque on March 24, 1810, when he was just 48 years of age. He died bankrupt, despite what had seemed the vast promise of his lands just a few decades earlier. Described by contemporaries as intelligent, well spoken, and ambitious, Dubuque undoubtedly was able to convince Chouteau and other merchants to extend him much more credit than he was able to repay.

While historical perspective makes Dubuque's treatment of his Indian friends look shady or downright crooked, the Native Americans still loved and respected him at the time of his death. They buried him with all the honors they would normally accord a chief. His burial site was located on the bluffs overlooking the Mississippi, not far from the city that now bears his name. The Fox people built a monument over his grave. In 1897, this building was replaced by a stone tower that still serves as a monument to his life.

Julien Dubuque's grave overlooks the Mississippi River.

After Dubuque's death, the Fox closed access to their lands. Pressure to open the lands to settlement grew as more and more settlers pushed west across the Mississippi. Following Black Hawk's War in 1832, virtually all of eastern Iowa was opened to white settlers.

If Dubuque had still been alive, he might have become a very rich man. As it was, the heirs of Auguste Chouteau waged a long legal battle to lay claim to the lands the St. Louis founder had been left by Dubuque. That battle was not settled until 1854, when the United States Supreme Court ruled against the Chouteau family.

Iowa from Dubuque to Statehood

For about two decades after the death of Dubuque, Native Americans controlled Iowa. In those years, land-hungry white settlers could only look at Iowa and dream of establishing settlements and farms, thanks to a treaty that forbid white settlers from crossing the Mississippi so long as the Indians held title to the lands.

By 1830, large numbers of these settlers were living on the Illinois side of the Mississippi River on land that had long been the hunting grounds of the Sauk. Their presence ultimately led to Black Hawk's War and the defeat of the Sauk and Fox. Over the next two decades, the Sauk, Fox, and other Native Americans were removed from Iowa to reservations in the west, their lands ceded to the United States. Only a few of these early inhabitants of Iowa remain in the state today.

Meanwhile, as the Native Americans left Iowa, white settlers moved in to take advantage of rich farmlands. In 1838, the region was organized as a U.S. territory. By 1840, the territory's population had reached 40,000, with most people living within about 50 miles of the Mississippi River.

Initially, the residents of Iowa Territory resisted the idea of statehood for a number of financial and political reasons. After reaching a compromise with the U.S. Congress about the state's boundaries, however, voters approved a state constitution. Iowa became the 29th state of the Union on December 28, 1846.

The growing town of Dubuque sketched in 1846, the year Iowa became a state

Black Hawk's War

Born in 1767, Black Hawk was a great leader of the Sauk. He refused to recognize a treaty signed by his people in 1804 giving the United States all the Sauk and Fox lands east of the Mississippi River in exchange for annual payments of $1,000.

In rejecting the agreement, Black Hawk declared that the U.S. government had taken advantage of five Sauk leaders who had come to St. Louis to turn in a warrior involved in the murder of three settlers. The land agreement was added on to the

Sauk warriors try to protect their families fleeing from U.S. soldiers at Bad Axe, Wisconsin. More than 300 Indians were ruthlessly killed during this battle in the summer of 1832.

negotiations about the warrior—after the chiefs were served a steady supply of alcohol.

Black Hawk participated in a number of skirmishes against U.S. soldiers and fought with the British in the War of 1812. Unrest continued until several violent incidents in 1827 prompted the federal government to remove all Indian tribes from Illinois. Black Hawk and his followers refused to give up their ancestral land of Saukenuk on the Mississippi River (today, Rock Island, Illinois). They farmed there peacefully during the summer of 1829, side by side with white settlers. But when the band returned from their winter hunt in 1830, the militia was called in to evict them.

Black Hawk left, but anger spread and grew. Other tribes, including the Fox, Winnebago, Kickapoo, and Potawatomi, joined Black Hawk, and in April 1832 they headed once again to Saukenuk. Federal troops were waiting. With only 40 men, Black Hawk won the first battle, but by the end of the summer his band was on the run across Wisconsin to the Mississippi River. After one failed river crossing, Black Hawk implored his people to follow him north. Only 50 did. U.S. troops caught up with the remaining Indians as they attempted to cross the river a second time. An estimated 300 men, women, and children died in the Massacre at Bad Axe. Black Hawk was later caught and jailed until he agreed to recognize Keokuk, who had signed away most of his people's land, as sole chief of the Sauks. Black Hawk died in 1838.

Keokuk, or the Watching Fox, succeeded Black Hawk, but was not a successful leader of the Sauk. He gave away most of his people's land.

Chapter Seven

Josiah & Abigail Snelling
the
First Family of Minnesota

I n 1824, General Winfield Scott, a hero of the War of 1812 who would eventually be a candidate for the office of president of the United States, wrote a letter to the U.S. War Department in Washington, D.C. At that time, Scott was inspecting a nearly completed fort being built on a limestone bluff overlooking the junction of the Mississippi and Minnesota Rivers.

"I wish to suggest to the general-in-chief and through him to the War Department, the propriety of calling this work Fort Snelling as a just compliment to the meritorious officer under whom it has been erected," Scott wrote.

The man to whom Scott referred in his letter was 42-year-old Colonel Josiah Snelling. Like Scott, Snelling was a military hero. Just one year later, the

Abigail Hunt Snelling (1797-1888) and Josiah Snelling (1783-1828) built an outpost designed to secure the territory of Minnesota for other settlers.

Winfield Scott (1788-1866) later became general-in-chief of the U.S. Army, serving from 1841 to 1861.

fort's name was changed from Fort St. Anthony—the name it had been given when it was first planned—to Fort Snelling.

Josiah Snelling Jr. was born in Boston, Massachusetts, sometime in 1783, just as the Revolutionary War was coming to an end. Red-headed Josiah was the 12th of 13 children of a prominent Boston baker, also named Josiah, and his wife, Mary Whitlock Snelling.

Josiah Jr. was born into a patriotic family. In the early months of the American Revolution, when Boston was in the hands of the British, Bostonians were forced to open their homes to the occupying enemy soldiers. Josiah's mother threw a British soldier who was rude to her out of the house. Not long after that, the elder Josiah Snelling refused to supply bread for the British army. As a result of their open support of the rebel cause, they were forced to flee the town until it was once again in the hands of the colonists.

In 1804, Josiah Snelling Jr. married Elizabeth Bell, who gave birth to a son, William Joseph Snelling, in December. Josiah worked at his father's bakery and was a member of the Massachusetts militia, a local force made up of volunteer soldiers. He received a commission as first lieutenant in the Fourth Infantry Division of the United States Army in 1808. That same year, Josiah and Elizabeth had a second son, who they named after his father. The child died in 1809, and then Elizabeth died the following year. Josiah sent his five-year-old son, William, to live with relatives.

Described as "a convivial, intelligent man of large spirit and incisive wit," Josiah Snelling found success as a soldier. In 1811, a series of battles was fought between the U.S. Army and a confederation of Native Americans led by Tecumseh, the great Shawnee chief. Angered by the loss of their land to the white settlers, Tecumseh had gathered warriors from many tribes to fight. In early November of that year, during the famous Battle of Tippecanoe, Snelling led a small group of men against a contingent of Indians who had taken cover in a grove of trees and were raking mounted soldiers with withering rifle fire. An earlier attack by another company

Snelling helped defeat the Shawnee, led by Tecumseh's brother The Prophet, at the Battle of Tippecanoe.

had failed, resulting in a large number of casualties, but Snelling and his soldiers drove the Indians from cover with the loss of just one man.

By June 1812, the United States was formally at war with Britain. Many Indians, resentful of their loss at Tippecanoe and the continuing encroachments into their land, aided the British. Now a captain, Snelling was assigned to the army post at Detroit in July 1812. Not long after Snelling arrived, he was introduced to Abigail Hunt, the daughter of Colonel Thomas Hunt, who had commanded the fort at Detroit from 1803 to 1806. Abigail's father and mother had died in 1808 and 1809, respectively, and she was living in Detroit with her brother, Henry, and his family when she met Josiah. They married less than two months later.

The couple had only a little time to enjoy their status as newlyweds. In August 1812, the British and their Indian allies attacked Detroit. The fort's commander, General William Hull, surrendered. Captured by the British when Detroit fell, Snelling and 2,000 other soldiers were sent to Montreal as prisoners of war. There Snelling displayed the same defiance of the British that both his mother and father had shown during the Revolutionary War. Marched past a monument to Lord Horatio Nelson, the great British admiral and naval hero, Snelling refused to remove his hat as a sign of respect.

Luckily for Snelling, he wasn't punished for what his captors must have seen as an act of insolence. As was the custom in wars in the past, he was soon paroled—sent home, but not allowed to fight

The first governor of Michigan Territory, William Hull (1753-1825) was court-martialed for cowardice and neglect of duty following his surrender of Detroit in 1812. Only his brilliant military record in the Revolutionary War saved him from execution.

against the British. Later, he was "exchanged" for a British prisoner of war of equal rank, and both men were once again allowed to fight. After this, Snelling served as a major and then a lieutenant colonel in the 4th Rifle Company of the army. He was stationed in Vermont and upstate New York.

The U.S. Army was sharply reduced in size at the end of the War of 1812, and many officers were forced to return to civilian life. Snelling, however, remained on active duty. At the war's end, he was promoted to the rank of lieutenant-colonel and then, in 1819, was made a full colonel.

In that same year, the Fifth Infantry was dispatched by Secretary of War John C. Calhoun to establish a series of forts that would give the U.S. control of what was then the northwest frontier. Soon after President Thomas Jefferson completed the Louisiana Purchase, he had sent General Zebulon Pike to explore the upper Mississippi River and Minnesota wilderness. In 1805, Pike had purchased from the Native Americans what was then a remote site on a point of land between the Mississippi River and the Minnesota River (at that time, called the St. Peter River). Now the U.S. realized the importance of a military presence in the region to protect settlers pressing ever westward in search of land.

In May 1819, the regiment departed for the frontier under the leadership of Lieutenant Colonel Henry Leavenworth, another hero of the War of 1812. For the next 12 weeks, Leavenworth and a

John Caldwell Calhoun (1782-1850) served as secretary of war from 1817 to 1825. A strong nationalist, he worked to build the country's military.

President Thomas Jefferson (1743-1826) sent military officers to explore the vast land acquired from France in the Louisiana Purchase.

Minnesota before the Snellings

When the first Europeans came to Minnesota in the second half of the seventeenth century, they found a beautiful land inhabited by a Native American people known as the Santee. These Indians were members of a larger group known collectively to Europeans as the Sioux. Hunters and farmers, the Sioux of Minnesota lived in dome-shaped wigwams. Large numbers of Ojibwa Indians later moved westward into Minnesota from their original hunting grounds around Lake Superior. As the Ojibwa moved into the region, they forced the Sioux to move southwest.

An Indian village on the Mississippi River, as painted by Seth Eastman

Two French fur traders, Pierre Esprit Radisson and Médard Chouart, sieur des Groseilliers, became the first Europeans to set foot in Minnesota in about 1660, when they explored the region in search of furs.

About 20 years after Radisson and Groseilliers entered Minnesota, another famous Frenchman, Daniel Greysolon, sieur Duluth (or Du Lhut), visited the region. Duluth, for whom the city of Duluth, Minnesota, was named, landed on the western shore of Lake Superior, and then pressed on into the interior of Minnesota. He claimed the entire area for King Louis XIV of France.

In 1762, as the French and Indian War neared its end, France gave Spain all its land west of the Mississippi River, including much of Minnesota, in an effort to keep the land out of British hands. The Spaniards, however, never settled the region or took advantage of its riches, and French trappers continued to collect furs there. In 1763, when the French and Indian War ended with the defeat of France, Britain gained control of most French land east of the Mississippi, including what is now northeastern Minnesota.

This section of Minnesota became part of the Northwest Territory after the end of the Revolutionary War. Meanwhile, in 1800, Napoleon Bonaparte of France forced Spain to return the formerly French lands west of the Mississippi River. In 1803, desperate for funds to wage wars in Europe, France sold this region, called Louisiana, to the United States in what was known as the Louisiana Purchase.

In 1819, the U.S. Army established a temporary fort where the Minnesota and Mississippi Rivers meet. The Snelling family would soon make its contribution to the settlement of Minnesota.

Explorer Duluth landing on the western shore of Lake Superior

DANIEL GREYSOLON SIEUR DULHUT
AT THE HEAD OF THE LAKES — 1679

Colonel Henry Leavenworth (1783-1834), who started work on Fort Snelling before Josiah Snelling took command, wrote this about the winter of 1819: "The mercury is 10 below zero and the ink freezes in my pen while I write. . . ." In 1825, Leavenworth established the fort that bears his name on the Missouri River in Kansas.

force of about 100 men, their families, and two dozen boatmen made a difficult journey.

The group left Detroit, traveling through Lakes Huron and Michigan to Fort Howard at Green Bay, Wisconsin. They then traveled by river through Wisconsin to Prairie du Chien on the Mississippi River. After resting, they turned north again, traveling upriver to where the Mississippi and Minnesota Rivers meet, arriving on August 24, 1819. During the following year, Leavenworth made only a halfhearted attempt to build a fort in a place he— and those with him—found barely inhabitable. Mosquitoes thrived in the low ground by the

Minnesota River, infecting the men with malaria. During the winter, they suffered from scurvy.

In the summer of 1820, Josiah Snelling was assigned as the unit's commander. By August he and his family had arrived in Prairie du Chien. Delayed there by supply problems, Snelling sent Henry Leavenworth notification that he was on his way. He asked that materials be collected for building a permanent post and remarked—in a slap at

Fort Snelling's strategic rivers-junction location and the cities that would later grow nearby, Minneapolis and St. Paul

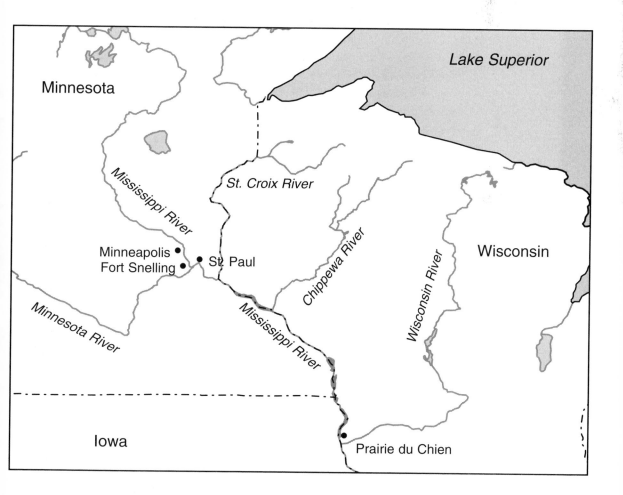

Leavenworth—that "it is not too late to complete it [the fort] this season."

In September 1820, the Snellings arrived at the fort with their two children, Mary, born in 1813, and Henry, born in 1816, plus William, Josiah's son from his first marriage. Abigail was pregnant at the time and two months later had a baby girl, Eliza. Sadly, Eliza lived for only 13 months.

Almost immediately after their arrival, Josiah Snelling oversaw the start of construction of the first permanent building to be erected on the new site of the fort, which had been relocated to a high bluff on the northwest bank of the junction of the two rivers. It took five years for the fort to be finished. Construction was delayed by a lack of supplies and of trained builders, and by Minnesota's long winters. At one point, a newly built hospital stood empty for an entire winter season because there were no nails to complete its roof.

Situated on a bluff overlooking the two rivers it guarded, the fort was constructed in the shape of a rough pentagon, with unequal sides. Its walls, built of stone quarried by the soldiers, stood between 12 and 14 feet high and were strong enough to withstand Indian attack. Within these walls stood barracks for enlisted men and officers, a school, a hospital, a trading post, a gun shed, a well that supplied the fort's inhabitants with fresh water, storehouses for guns and powder, and a large commandant's house where the Snelling family lived.

By 1825 the fort was finished. The simple fact that a fort had been raised in such harsh conditions

Fort Snelling commanded a clear view of both rivers and the surrounding area.

was something of a miracle. It was especially remarkable given the fact that Snelling had to recruit all his help—including his architect—from the men in his own regiment. Lawrence Taliaferro, the Indian agent assigned to the fort, wrote that the fort had been "reared as if by magic in the forest wilds."

Snelling must have felt a sense of accomplishment as he looked over what was, in a real sense, his domain. And he had reason to feel proud. Not only had he overseen the construction of a frontier citadel, but he had also ordered a flour mill to be built at the Falls of St. Anthony, on the Mississippi River north of the fort. Under Snelling's direction, land just outside the fort's walls was cleared and garden vegetables were grown. Livestock, including cattle, were bred to supply the fort's inhabitants with meat.

Life in the fort was still not easy. In the 1820s, Fort Snelling—located at the far western edge of the northwestern frontier—was almost completely isolated. The Mississippi River provided the only contact those in the fort had with the outside world. During the long winter, the river was iced over and impassable. In the spring, the Mississippi became a watery highway that ensured the delivery of mail and newspapers as well as visitors. At the same time, the river was often packed with ice floes and sometimes overflowed its banks, flooding the fort's lower floors and drowning horses, cattle, and even—one year when the floods were especially bad—Snelling's clerk. The winter of 1826 was particularly harsh and melting snows sent the river far over its banks. "The

In an effort to make the fort self-sufficient, Snelling had his men plant crops, including corn, near the fort. Each year, though, much of the corn crop was destroyed by blackbirds. "I am weary of crying out the blackbirds, the blackbirds," he wrote, "but . . . in a few days they destroy the labour of months."

two rivers have subsided but very little," Snelling wrote in May of that year. "The whole country in front of the garrison is a lake. All our boats were lost. We have had not spring; not a plow or spade has yet been put in the ground, nor a seed sown."

The Falls of St. Anthony provided the power to mill grain, and the city of Minneapolis grew up next to them. Father Louis Hennepin, shown here, was the first European to see and name the falls.

Despite Snelling's attempts to make the outpost self-sufficient, those in the fort were dependent upon food and other supplies from the army. Because of its location, delivery of needed supplies to the fort by river was uncertain under the best of circumstances. At one point in 1827, the situation at what Snelling called his "garrison" was so desperate that Snelling considered abandoning the post. Two years later, supply boats delayed for weeks by low water arrived when the fort was down to its last barrel of flour. Snelling, after pleading for new uniforms for himself for three years without any response, became so embarrassed by his bedraggled appearance that he refused to appear before his men.

Still, not all at the frontier fort was hardship. Abigail Snelling created a pleasant home for the colonel in the commandant's quarters. Their house, perched on a bluff overlooking the Mississippi, was luxurious by frontier standards, with four fireplaces and plenty of room for the couple's family. Abigail, no doubt happy for the chance to entertain, missed no opportunity to play hostess for dignitaries and Native American chiefs who came to visit. She also hosted dinner parties for the younger officers on the post. Snelling, who was called "the Prairie Chicken" by his men because of his sparse, red hair that often stood on end, enjoyed those parties, where he was able to entertain the younger officers with humorous stories.

Though there were only a few women at the isolated post, the soldiers also passed time by arranging dances and band concerts. Snelling arranged to

Fort Snelling was beset by supply problems from its earliest days. Snelling became a master at improvisation. One year, when he ran out of paper and forms needed to report to his superiors, he sent his reports in on cartridge paper used in his soldiers' muskets.

have books sent to the fort and established a library with some 400 volumes. Hunting and fishing expeditions were made when the weather was pleasant. In the winter, ice skating and sleigh rides made life a little more enjoyable.

An interior view of Fort Snelling

As part of the food ration, each soldier was given a gill (about half a cup) of whisky each day. Many of the men, lonely in the wilderness and bored by duty that was both tedious and difficult, turned to drink. Court-martials for intoxication were common in what the post surgeon described as an "empire of drunkenness."

During Snelling's time as commander of the fort, he was, in fact, dissatisfied with many of the recruits sent to serve on the frontier. More than a few were convicts who were offered pardons for their service; others were alcoholics, old men who could find no other work, or men physically unfit for service. "The . . . last detachment of recruits from N. York were the greatest vagabonds I ever saw," Josiah Snelling wrote in 1825. "I have almost been inclined to think that the best men are kept on the seaboard and this post made a kind of Botany bay for the reception of those who can live no where else." (Botany Bay was an English prison colony established in what is now New Zealand.)

Even more troubling was a new breed of officers being sent west. These men had graduated from West Point, the new U.S. military academy, and they looked down on the old soldier who had come up through the ranks. Not surprisingly, morale in the fort started to decline. "[Q]uarreling, tattleing—neglect of military duty, and a total absence of all the finer feelings" were commonplace within the fort's walls, said Indian Agent Taliaferro.

By early 1826, the harshness of life on the frontier, probably coupled with disappointment about the situation in the fort, took its toll on Josiah Snelling. His health broke. Prescribed opium and brandy, he soon spun out of control. Though Snelling remained at the fort until late 1827, his last

Boredom was a constant companion for the soldiers at Fort Snelling. From the earliest days of the fort, plays were staged by the soldiers, with men playing the women's parts. One soldier urged his companions to take advantage of the plays: "In a short time we shall be assailed by all the rigors of a northern winter," he wrote. "Something that will engage our attention and divert our minds from this state of things, and at the same time afford amusement, cannot surely be treated with neglect and indifference."

The Sioux called Lawrence Taliaferro "No-sugar-in-your-mouth" because of his honest dealings with them. Taliaferro and Snelling had fought together during the War of 1812. Reunited by their work at the fort, they became good friends and respected colleagues.

months there must have been miserable. His judgment impaired, he was involved in several duels and, eventually, in a series of court-martials and civil lawsuits that threatened to end his career in disgrace.

In October 1827, he left the fort he founded for good. Less than a year later, on August 20, 1828, he died in Washington, D.C., where he had been living with his brother-in-law, Thomas Hunt. Snelling was survived by his wife, Abigail, and four of their children, as well as by William, the son of his first marriage. According to one of his fellow officers, Snelling died because "his constitution [was] broken by his arduous and laborious services" on the frontier.

Snelling assessed his career with a modest eye. "I have passed through every grade to the command of a regiment," he said. "I have obtained my rank in the ordinary course of promotion, and have retained it by doing my duty." The fort he had built was renamed in his honor in January 1825. In the years following Snelling's departure from the banks of the Mississippi, the "Twin Cities" of Minneapolis and St. Paul grew up around the fort in the wilderness.

Abigail Snelling would live another 60 years. After Josiah's death, she returned to Michigan, first living on the farm Josiah had owned, and later moving to Detroit, where she ran a boarding house. Among her boarders was Jonathan E. Chaplin, a Methodist minister whom she married in 1841. They lived in Ohio at first, and then returned to Michigan. Chaplin died in 1846, leaving Abigail a widow once more. She then lived in Cincinnati with her son James, who had fought in the Mexican War. Following his death in 1855, she lived with her daughter Marion. For 18 frustrating years, she attempted to collect a widow's pension from the government. In 1873, she was finally granted $30 per month in recognition of Josiah's service to his country. Abigail died on September 6, 1888.

The city of Minneapolis stretches toward the skies. Minneapolis is located on the west bank of the Mississippi River; its "twin city" of St. Paul was built farther south on the east bank. Although slightly less in population, St. Paul can boast being the state capital.

Minnesota from Settlement to Statehood

In the years after the establishment of Fort Snelling, several treaties signed with the Ojibwa and the Sioux gave the U.S. government control of Native American lands and led to a rapid increase in population as farmers and other settlers moved into the region.

In 1848, when Wisconsin was admitted to the Union as a state, several thousand settlers living between the Mississippi and

Almost all the old-growth trees in Minnesota were cut for timber, creating great wealth for a few lumber barons. The lumber industry continues to be an important one, although the trees cut in the early twenty-first century are from second- or third-growth forests or tree farms.

St. Croix Rivers were left without any government representation. In response to their needs, a one-day convention was held at Stillwater, Minnesota. At that convention, delegates chose Henry H. Sibley, the regional director of the American Fur Company, to represent the Minnesota settlers in Congress. Sibley soon introduced legislation calling for the creation of the Minnesota Territory. The Minnesota Territorial Act became law on March 3, 1849.

The new territory attracted thousands of settlers with its rich farmlands and thick forests. The land boom increased as new towns were plotted and roads and railroads pushed their way into the frontier. In the years between 1850 and 1857, the territory's population soared from about 6,000 to about 150,000.

This increase in population led to a move for statehood in 1856. Voters approved a constitution in a general election in October 1857, and Minnesota was admitted to the Union as the 32nd state on May 11, 1858.

Henry H. Sibley (1811-1891) became Minnesota's first governor.

North and South Dakota

The first inhabitants of the region that eventually became the states of North and South Dakota were Native Americans. As was the case with other native people in the Midwest, these early residents were descendants of people who migrated into the region many thousands of years ago.

Native Americans who lived in the region included members of farming tribes such as the Mandan and Hidatsa in North Dakota and the Arikara, who lived in both states. Other groups who lived in the area included the Cheyenne, Crow, Ojibwa, and Cree in North Dakota, and the Sioux in both North and South Dakota. Originally from the forests, the Sioux were pushed into the Dakotas when the Ojibwa moved into Minnesota. In their new grasslands home, the Sioux adopted a nomadic life that revolved around hunting buffalo.

Sioux hunters and their ponies race across the Dakota grasslands in pursuit of buffalo. The animals provided the Sioux with food, clothing, shelter, and tools.

In 1682, René Robert Cavelier, sieur de La Salle, the famous French adventurer, explored the Mississippi River and claimed all the lands drained by that river for France, including the Dakotas. During much of the next century, those lands remained under French control. While nominally the "property" of France, the region was not actually visited by any European until 1738, when Pierre Gaultier de Varennes, sieur de La Verendrye, passed through North Dakota while searching for the fabled Northwest Passage.

A few years later, Louis-Joseph and François Gaultier, Pierre Gaultier's sons, along with two other French explorers, made an epic journey deep into the north-central region, again in hopes of reaching the "western sea." In the course of their 15-month journey of exploration, they reached what are thought to have been the Big Horn Mountains in Wyoming, then returned along the Cheyenne and Bad Rivers, eventually reaching what is now Pierre, South Dakota. There the explorers buried a lead plaque that was not discovered until 1915.

The region that includes the Dakotas remained in French hands until 1762, when France gave it to Spain in an effort to keep the region and other lands out of British control in the wake of the French and Indian War. In 1800, Spain returned

A statue of Pierre Gaultier de Varennes, sieur de La Verendrye

the lands to France, which was by that time in need of money to pay for its wars in Europe. In 1803, when the United States and French governments concluded the Louisiana Purchase, some of North Dakota and all of South Dakota became part of the U.S. In 1818, the remainder of North Dakota became part of the U.S. when the border between the United States and Canada was fixed at the 49th parallel.

When the Lewis and Clark expedition to explore the lands west of the Mississippi River returned to the East in 1805, the explorers told of vast herds of buffalo and other fur-bearing animals to be found in the Dakotas. For a half-century following that expedition, hunting and trapping

Meriwether Lewis and William Clark wintered with the Mandan Indians in North Dakota in 1804-1805 before beginning their trek west.

The fort at Pembina as it must have looked in the early 1800s

dominated the region. During those years, buffalo vanished from the plains. Beaver, whose pelts were popular for hats, were all but wiped out in the region's rivers.

At the same time, the Dakotas became home to numerous fur-trading and army posts. The first serious attempt at permanent settlement was made by Alexander Henry at Pembina, North Dakota, in 1801. This attempt failed, however, and it was not until 1851 that a permanent settlement was established, also at Pembina.

In South Dakota, meanwhile, settlement in the early nineteenth century was limited to the trading posts founded by individual fur traders and trappers. The most notable of these was Fort Pierre, founded by Pierre Chouteau and the American Fur Company in 1817. This fort eventually grew to be the city of Pierre (pronounced "Peer"), the state capital of South Dakota.

While the Dakotas were attractive to those involved in the fur industry, true settlement of the region did not begin until the mid-nineteenth century, when it became apparent that the region would one day become a U.S. territory. Some farmers and land speculators were moving into both North and South Dakota. One of the reasons for the slow pace of settlement was the fairly constant conflict between whites and Native Americans, particularly the Sioux. In 1859, however, a treaty between the U.S. government and the Sioux opened land in the Dakotas for settlement. The cities of Yankton, Bon Homme, and Vermillion in South Dakota were laid out, and in 1861 the Dakota Territory was established. This territory included parts of Wyoming and Montana as well as the Dakotas. Yankton was the capital.

While some brave pioneer men and women moved into the Dakota Territory in the years immediately following its establishment, the pace of settlement was slow. The land was rich, but the climate was harsh, and droughts and locusts were not uncommon. Then, in 1872, the railroad reached Yankton, bringing many immigrants. Two years later, gold was discovered in the Black Hills of South Dakota. Sacred to the Indians, the Black Hills had been guaranteed to the Sioux, but the gold tempted many whites to violate the treaty.

(Jean) Pierre Chouteau (1758-1849)

states of the Union. By this time, the buffalo herds that the Sioux had depended upon were gone. The following year, their great chief Sitting Bull died and more than 200 Sioux, including women and children, were massacred at Wounded Knee Creek in South Dakota when government troops attacked. The resistance was over.

Many immigrant families traveled west to the prairies by train during the late 1800s.

Fortune hunters poured into the region, leading to renewed war between the Sioux and the settlers.

Ultimately, Native American efforts to stem the flow of settlement failed. Settlers voted to divide the territory in half in 1887, and on November 2, 1889, North and South Dakota became the 39th and 40th

Sitting Bull (1831?-1890) was one of the Sioux leaders during the Battle of the Little Bighorn, in which the Sioux killed George Armstrong Custer and all his men.

A Midwestern Timeline

1492: Christopher Columbus discovers North America.

1497-1498: John Cabot sails from Britain to Canada, exploring the North American coastline.

1535: Jacques Cartier discovers the St. Lawrence River, landing at a Huron village that becomes Montreal.

1603-1616: Samuel de Champlain sails past Montreal into upstate New York and explores Lakes Ontario and Huron.

1618: Étienne Brûlé reaches Michigan.

1634: Jean Nicolet, looking for the Northwest Passage, lands in Green Bay, Wisconsin.

March 5, 1658: Antoine Laumet de Lamothe Cadillac is born in France.

1659: Pierre Esprit Radisson and Médard Chouart, sieur des Groseilliers, journey through Lake Superior and become the first Europeans to reach Minnesota.

1668: Jacques Marquette founds a mission at Sault Saint Marie, Michigan; it is the first European settlement in that state.

1673: Louis Joliet and Jacques Marquette discover the Mississippi River.

1679: René Robert Cavelier, sieur de La Salle, sails into Green Bay, Wisconsin, aboard the *Griffon*, the first large vessel to navigate the Great Lakes.

1681-1682: La Salle journeys down the Mississippi River to the Gulf of Mexico.

1683: Cadillac arrives in Nova Scotia, Canada.

June 25, 1687: Cadillac marries Marie-Thérèse Guyon.

1687-1688: Henri Joutel explores near present-day Chicago.

1693: Cadillac receives command of Fort de Buade at Michilimackinac and begins charting the Great Lakes.

1696: Jesuit missionary François Pinet founds a mission to serve the Miami not far from Chicago. Four years later, he abandons the attempt.

1698: Cadillac proposes to King Louis XIV that a settlement be established on the Detroit River.

June 4, 1701: Cadillac lands at the site of Detroit, Michigan.

1710: Cadillac is appointed governor of Louisiana.

1718: Cadillac returns to France.

1720: The French build forts near Fort Wayne, Lafayette, and Vincennes, Indiana.

1729: Charles-Michel Mouet de Langlade is born in Michigan.

1730: Cadillac dies in France.

April 9, 1738: Rufus Putnam is born in Sutton, Massachusetts.

1738: Pierre Gaultier de Varennes, sieur de La Verendrye, travels through North Dakota.

1745: The year **Jean Baptiste Pointe du Sable** is most likely born in San Marc, Haiti.

June 1752: Langlade defeats the Miamis at Pickawillany.

November 18, 1752: George Rogers Clark is born in Virginia.

1754-1763: The French and Indian War is fought between Britain and France in North America.

1755: Langlade fights in the Battle of the Wilderness, an important battle in the French and Indian War.

1757-1760: Putnam joins the army and fights for the British during the French and Indian War.

1760: Michilimackinac falls to the British.

January 10, 1762: Julien Dubuque is born in Quebec.

February 10, 1763: The Treaty of Paris ends the French and Indian War, giving Britain control of all lands east of the Mississippi River.

1763-1765: Pontiac's War is waged by Ottawa chief Pontiac and an alliance of many Great Lakes tribes against the British.

1765: Langlade and his family settle in Green Bay, Wisconsin.

1765: Jean du Sable begins farming near Peoria, Illinois.

1775-1783: The American colonies fight for independence from Britain in the Revolutionary War.

1775: Putnam joins the Continental Army.

1776: Clark persuades the Virginia Assembly to make Kentucky part of Virginia and to aid the Kentuckians in their fight against the Native Americans.

1777: Virginia Governor Patrick Henry gives **Clark** supplies and secret orders to attack British-held forts in Illinois Territory.

1778: Clark and his men leave Fort Pitt, Pennsylvania, bound for Illinois and Indiana, where Clark hopes to capture British forts.

July 1778: Clark takes over British strongholds in Kaskaskia, Illinois, and Vincennes, Indiana.

February 25, 1779: After days of marching through freezing water with little to eat, **Clark** and his men retake control of the fort at Vincennes—an important victory during the Revolutionary War.

1779: Du Sable moves to Chicago and establishes a trading post there; he's arrested by the British and imprisoned briefly on Mackinac Island. Du Sable then works for a British colonel, helping him run a fort near Port Huron, Michigan.

1782: Dubuque arrives in the upper Mississippi River valley.

1783: The Treaty of Paris is signed, formally ending the Revolutionary War, and in it Great Britain cedes the Northwest Territory to the United States.

1783: Putnam drafts the Newburgh Petition, asking the government to give Revolutionary War veterans land in Ohio.

1783: Josiah Snelling is born in Boston, Massachusetts.

1784: Clark founds Clarksville, Indiana, on the Ohio River.

1784: **Du Sable** returns to Chicago.

May 20, 1785: The Land Ordinance is passed, establishing the basic unit of land— a township that is 36 square miles.

1785: **Putnam** forms the Ohio Company.

July 1787: The Northwest Ordinance establishes territorial government in the Northwest Territory (Ohio, Illinois, Indiana, Michigan, Wisconsin, and part of Minnesota) after the British cede this land.

October 1787: Congress appoints General Arthur St. Clair the first governor of the Northwest Territory.

December 3, 1787: A group of 47 men under **Rufus Putnam's** leadership leave Massachusetts to establish the first settlement in Ohio.

April 7, 1788: **Putnam's** party reaches Marietta, Ohio.

September 22, 1788: The Fox give **Dubuque** the right to mine lead on their land.

August 1794: General Anthony Wayne and his soldiers defeat the Indian forces at the Battle of Fallen Timbers in Ohio. One year later the Indians cede Ohio and most of Indiana.

1796: **Putnam** appointed surveyor general of the U.S.

1797: **Abigail Hunt** is born.

May 1800: **Du Sable** sells his home and business in Chicago and returns to Peoria.

1800: **Charles Langlade** dies.

1800: Indiana Territory is created.

1801: Alexander Henry establishes Pembina, the first permanent settlement in North Dakota.

March 1, 1803: Ohio becomes the nation's 17th state.

April 30, 1803: The United States buys the Louisiana Territory from France.

1803: Fort Dearborn constructed near **du Sable's** former trading post in Chicago.

1803: **Clark** returns to live in Clarksville, Indiana.

1804-1805: An expedition led by Meriwether Lewis and William Clark explores the Louisiana Territory and finds a land route to the Pacific Ocean.

1805: Michigan Territory created from the Indiana Territory.

1805: **Du Sable** moves to St. Charles, Missouri.

1805: Zebulon Pike purchases the site of the future Fort Snelling.

1808: **Snelling** begins his military career as a first lieutenant in the U.S. Army.

1809: Illinois Territory created from the Indiana Territory.

March 24, 1810: **Julien Dubuque** dies in the Iowa town that now bears his name.

November 6, 1811: At Tippecanoe, Indiana, General William Henry Harrison defeats the confederacy of Native Americans created by Tecumseh, who wanted a separate Indian nation in the Great Lakes region.

1812-1814: The United States fights Britain in the War of 1812.

July 1812: **Snelling** is assigned to the army post in Detroit.

August 1812: **Snelling** marries **Abigail Hunt**; Detroit falls soon after and **Snelling** briefly becomes a prisoner of war.

August 1812: Fort Dearborn is destroyed by Indians fighting for the British.

1816: Fort Howard is constructed in Green Bay, Wisconsin.

December 1, 1816: Indiana enters the Union as the 19th state.

1817: Fort Pierre, now Pierre, South Dakota, is founded by Pierre Chouteau and the American Fur Company.

1817: Fort Dearborn is reconstructed near Chicago.

February 13, 1818: **George Rogers Clark** dies in Louisville, Kentucky.

1818: **Du Sable** dies in Missouri.

1818: Wisconsin becomes part of the Michigan Territory.

December 3, 1818: Illinois becomes the 21st state.

August 24, 1819: A force led by Lieutenant Colonel Henry Leavenworth arrives at the junction of the Mississippi and Minnesota Rivers and attempts to build a fort there.

September 1820: **Josiah** and **Abigail Snelling** and their family arrive at the site of the proposed Minnesota fort.

May 4, 1824: **Rufus Putnam** dies in Marietta, Ohio.

1825: Fort Snelling is complete.

October 1827: **Josiah** and **Abigail Snelling** leave Fort Snelling.

August 20, 1828: **Josiah Snelling** dies in Washington, D.C.

1832: Black Hawk's War to regain his people's ancestral lands on the Mississippi River ends in a massacre and the loss of all Sauk territory.

1836: Part of the Michigan Territory is organized into the Wisconsin Territory.

January 26, 1837: Michigan becomes the 26th state.

1837: **Chicago** is chartered as a city.

1838: Iowa is organized as a U.S. territory.

December 28, 1846: Iowa becomes the nation's 29th state.

May 30, 1848: Wisconsin becomes the 30th state of the Union.

March 3, 1849: The Minnesota Territorial Act becomes law.

May 11, 1858: Minnesota becomes the 32nd state.

1859: A treaty between the U.S. government and the Sioux opens the Dakotas for settlement.

1861: The Dakota Territory is established.

1871: One-third of Chicago is destroyed by fire; 250 people die.

1873: After 18 years of trying to collect a widow's pension, **Abigail Snelling** is granted a monthly stipend in recognition of **Josiah**'s military service.

1874: Gold is discovered in the Black Hills of South Dakota, renewing war between the settlers and the Sioux.

1887: Settlers vote to divide the Dakota Territory in half.

September 6, 1888: **Abigail Snelling** dies.

November 2, 1889: North and South Dakota become the 39th and 40th states of the Union.

In 1825, more than 5,000 Native Americans from several different tribes came together in Prairie du Chien, Wisconsin (part of Michigan Territory at the time), to meet with Michigan governor Lewis Cass and William Clark, then an Indian agent. Hoping for peace, participants signed the Great Treaty, which laid out specific boundaries for tribes and settlers.

Source Notes

Quoted passages are noted by page and order of citation.

Chapter One

p. 20 (caption): Henry D. Brown, et al., *Cadillac and the Founding of Detroit* (Detroit: Wayne State University Press, 1976), 20.

p. 20: Brown, *Cadillac*, 49.

pp. 20-21: Brown, *Cadillac*, 21.

p. 21 (first margin): Brown, *Cadillac*, 23.

p. 21 (second margin): Brown, *Cadillac*, 19.

p. 23: Brown, *Cadillac*, 23.

p. 25 (margin): Brown, *Cadillac*, 60.

p. 25: Brown, *Cadillac*, 59.

p. 29 (margin): Brown, *Cadillac*, 69.

p. 29: Brown, *Cadillac*, 111.

Chapter Two

p. 37: Richard Nelson Current, *Wisconsin: A Bicentennial History* (New York: W. W. Norton, 1977), 4.

p. 49 (first): Fred Holmes, *Badger Saints and Sinners* (Milwaukee: E. M. Hale, 1936), 33.

p. 49 (second): Holmes, *Badger Saints*, 31.

Chapter Three

p. 54: Milo M. Quaife, *Checagou; from Indian Wigwam to Modern City, 1673-1835* (Chicago: University of Chicago Press, 1933), 36.

p. 61 (margin): John A. Garraty and Mark C. Carnes, eds., *American National Biography*, Vol. 7 (New York: Oxford University Press, 1999), 166.

p. 62: Quaife, *Checagou*, 37.

p. 63: Quaife, *Checagou*, 39.

p. 64 (caption): Garraty and Carnes, *American National Biography*, 166.

Chapter Four

p. 77: Theodore Roosevelt, *The Winning of the West*, Vol. 2 (Lincoln: University of Nebraska Press, 1995), 2.

p. 79 (margin): Milo M. Quaife, *The Capture of Old Vincennes: The Original Narratives of George Rogers Clark and of his Opponent Gov. Henry Hamilton* (Indianapolis: Bobbs-Merrill, 1927), 48.

p. 80 (first and second): George Rogers Clark, *Memoir* (Indiana Historical Bureau http://www.statelib.lib.in.us/www/ihb/grcmemtwo.html), 7.

p. 80 (third): Clark, *Memoir*, 10.

p. 83 (margin): John Edwin Bakeless, *Background to Glory: The Life of George Rogers Clark* (Philadelphia: Lippincott, 1957), 97.

p. 84 (caption): Bakeless, *Background to Glory*, 105.

p. 85 (first): Clark, *Memoir*, 2.

p. 85 (second): Clark, *Memoir*, 4.

p. 85 (third): Page Smith, *A New Age Now Begins: A People's History of the American Revolution*, Vol. 2 (New York: McGraw-Hill, 1976), 1203.

p. 85 (fourth): Smith, *A New Age*, 1205.

p. 87: Smith, *A New Age*, 1233.

Chapter Five

p. 95 (margin): Ted Morgan, *Wilderness at Dawn: The Settling of the North American Continent* (New York: Simon & Schuster, 1993), 411.

p. 100: Morgan, *Wilderness at Dawn*, 412.

p. 101 (first): *The Founders of Ohio* (Cincinnati: Robert Clark, 1888), 7.

p. 101 (second): *Founders*, 5.

p. 101 (third and fourth): *Founders*, 6.

p. 103 (first): Morgan, *Wilderness at Dawn*, 406.

p. 103 (second): Morgan, *Wilderness at Dawn*, 417.

p. 108 (margin): Morgan, *Wilderness at Dawn*, 462.

p. 109 (margin): Morgan, *Wilderness at Dawn*, 437.

Chapter Six

p. 117 (first): Thomas Auge, "The Life and Times of Julien Dubuque," *Palimpsest Magazine*, Jan./Feb. 1976 (Iowa City: Iowa State Historical Department), 2.

p. 117 (second): Auge, "Julien Dubuque," 3.

p. 118 (margin): Auge, "Julien Dubuque," 6.

p. 118: Auge, "Julien Dubuque," 5.

p. 121: Garraty and Carnes, *American National Biography*, 1.

Chapter Seven

p. 131: Stephen P. Hall, *Fort Snelling, Colossus of the Wilderness* (St. Paul: Minnesota Historical Society Press, 1987), xx.

p. 133: Hall, *Fort Snelling*, 15.

p. 138 (caption): Ted Morgan, *A Shovel of Stars: The Making of the American West, 1800 to the Present* (New York: Simon & Schuster, 1995), 184.

p. 139: Hall, *Fort Snelling*, 16.

p. 142 (margin): Hall, *Fort Snelling*, 21.

p. 142: Hall, *Fort Snelling*, 17.

pp. 142-143: Hall, *Fort Snelling*, 20.

p. 144: Dumas Malone, ed., *Dictionary of American Biography*, Vol. IX (New York: Scribners, 1964), 381.

p. 145: Hall, *Fort Snelling*, 25.

p. 146 (margin): Hall, *Fort Snelling*, 25.

p. 146 (first): Morgan, *A Shovel of Stars*, 185.

p. 146 (second): Hall, *Fort Snelling*, 26.

p. 147 (caption): Hall, *Fort Snelling*, 23.

p. 148 (first): Hall, *Fort Snelling*, 26.

p. 148 (second): Malone, *Dictionary*, 381.

Bibliography

Anderson, Fred. *Crucible of War: The Seven Years' War and the Fate of Empire in British North America, 1754-1766.* New York: Alfred A. Knopf, 2000.

Auge, Thomas. "The Life and Times of Julien Dubuque." *Palimpsest Magazine*, Jan./Feb. 1976. Iowa City: Iowa State Historical Department.

Bakeless, John Edwin. *America as Seen by Its First Explorers: The Eyes of Discovery.* Mineola, N.Y.: Dover, 1961.

———. *Background to Glory: The Life of George Rogers Clark.* Philadelphia: Lippincott, 1957.

Boorstin, Daniel J. *The Americans: The Colonial Experience.* New York: Random House, 1958.

———. *The Americans: The Democratic Experience.* New York: Random House, 1973.

———. *The Americans: The National Experience.* New York: Random House, 1965.

Brown, Henry D., et al. *Cadillac and the Founding of Detroit.* Detroit: Wayne State University Press, 1976.

Clark, George Rogers. *Memoir.* Indiana Historical Bureau. Online at http://www.statelib.lib.in.us/www/ihb/grcmemtwo.html.

Current, Richard Nelson. *Wisconsin: A Bicentennial History.* New York: W. W. Norton, 1977.

Davis, James E. *Frontier Illinois.* Bloomington: Indiana University Press, 1998.

English, William Hayden. *Conquest of the Country Northwest of the River Ohio 1778-1783 and Life of Gen. George Rogers Clark.* Indianapolis: Bowen-Merrill, 1897. Online at http://www.statelib.lib.in.us/WWW/IHB/grcbio.html.

The Founders of Ohio. Cincinnati: Robert Clark, 1888.

Gara, Larry. *A Short History of Wisconsin*. Madison: The State Historical Society of Wisconsin, 1962.

Garraty, John A. and Mark C. Carnes, eds. *American National Biography*. New York: Oxford University Press, 1999.

Hall, Stephen P. *Fort Snelling, Colossus of the Wilderness*. St. Paul: Minnesota Historical Society Press, 1987.

Holmes, Fred. *Badger Saints and Sinners*. Milwaukee: E. M. Hale, 1936.

James, James Alton, ed. *George Rogers Clark Papers*, Volume VIII. Springfield: Illinois State Historical Society Library, 1912.

Luecke, Barbara K. and John C. *Snelling: Minnesota's First First Family*. Eagan, Minn.: Grenadia, 1993.

Malone, Dumas, ed. *Dictionary of American Biography*. New York: Scribners, 1964.

Minks, Benton and Louise. *The French and Indian War*. San Diego: Lucent Books, 1995.

Morgan, Ted. *A Shovel of Stars: The Making of the American West, 1800 to the Present*. New York: Simon & Schuster, 1995.

———. *Wilderness at Dawn: The Settling of the North American Continent*. New York: Simon & Schuster, 1993.

Morison, Samuel Eliot, Henry Steele Commager, and William E. Leuchtenburg. *The Growth of the American Republic*. New York: Oxford University Press, 1980.

Nesbit, Roger C. and William F. Thompson. *Wisconsin: A History*. Madison: University of Wisconsin Press, 1989.

Quaife, Milo M. *The Capture of Old Vincennes: The Original Narratives of George Rogers Clark and of his Opponent Gov. Henry Hamilton.* Indianapolis: Bobbs-Merrill, 1927.

———. *Checagou; from Indian Wigwam to Modern City, 1673-1835.* Chicago: University of Chicago Press, 1933.

Quinn, Arthur. *A New World: An Epic of Colonial America from the Founding of Jamestown to the Fall of Quebec.* Boston: Faber & Faber, 1994.

Roosevelt, Theodore. *The Winning of the West,* Volume 2. Lincoln: University of Nebraska Press, 1995.

Smith, Page. *A New Age Now Begins: A People's History of the American Revolution,* Volume 2. New York: McGraw-Hill, 1976.

Thomas, Lowell. *The Hero of Vincennes: The Story of George Rogers Clark.* Boston: Houghton Mifflin, 1929.

Waldman, Carl. *Atlas of the North American Indian.* New York: Facts on File, 1985.

Index

France, 18, 20, 21, 23, 29, 30, 122; as American ally during Revolutionary War, 80, 82; explorers of, in New World, 9, 10, 11, 12, 22, 37, 47, 48, 55, 56, 57-59, 78, 114, 116, 136, 153; in French and Indian Wars, 13, 35, 42, 44, 45, 77, 94, 99, 116, 136; in fur trade, 13, 23, 24, 26, 32, 47, 78, 114, 116, 136; relationships of, with Native Americans, 40, 42, 44, 47, 94, 99; sale of Louisiana to U.S., 122, 135, 137, 154; territories of, 18, 19, 32, 122, 153

Franklin, Benjamin, 88

French and Indian Wars, 14, 35, 36, 45, 94, 95, 116, 136, 153; British victory in, 13, 32, 42, 44, 99, 136; causes of, 44, 99

Frontenac, Fort, 59

Frontenac, Louis de Buade, comte de, 21, 25, 57

fur trade, 22, 35, 37, 38, 48, 49, 123; beaver pelts in, 23, 37, 114, 155; British role in, 32, 51, 74, 78; in Dakotas, 154-155, 156; as factor in French and Indian Wars, 44, 99; French role in, 13, 23, 24, 26, 32, 47, 78, 114, 116, 136; Native Americans in, 13, 23, 24, 55, 56, 98-99

Gaultier, François, 153

Gaultier, Louis-Joseph, 153

Gaultier de Varennes, Pierre, sieur de La Verendrye, 153

General Motors Company, 31

George III (king of England), 74

Ghent, Treaty of, 91

Gibault, Pierre, 82

Gladwin, Henry, 46

gold, discovered in Black Hills, 156

Great Britain, 9, 74; in French and Indian Wars, 13, 32, 35, 42, 44, 45, 77, 94, 99, 153; in fur trade, 32, 51, 74, 78; relationships of, with Native Americans, 32, 36, 40, 69, 77, 90, 91, 99, 129, 134; in Revolutionary War, 14, 45, 47, 51, 61, 68, 71-72, 77, 82, 83, 86, 87, 96, 97, 99, 132; territories of, 13, 19, 32, 44, 102, 116, 122, 136; in War of 1812, 32, 51, 69, 90, 91, 129, 134, 135

Great Lakes, 2, 33, 78, 88, 90, 97, 98; exploration of, 10, 21, 23, 37, 59; French control of, 9, 13, 19, 26, 29, 39; Native Americans in region of, 12-13, 22, 45; trade on, 13, 38, 57, 63, 67. See also individual lakes

Green Bay, 37, 48, 50, 57, 138; settlement at, 14, 36, 47, 49, 51

Green Bay Packers, 50

Griffon, 47, 48

Groseilliers, Médard Chouart, sieur des, 11, 37, 136

Guyon, François, 19, 20

Hamilton, Henry, 77, 83, 84, 86, 87

Harrison, William Henry, 90, 91, 110, 123

Helm, Leonard, 83

Hennepin, Louis, 7, 143

Henry, Alexander, 155

Henry, Patrick, 75, 76, 79

Hidatsa Indians, 152

Hochelaga, 9, 10

Hopewell culture, 78

Hopkins, Frances Anne, 2

Howard, Fort, 49, 50, 138

Hull, William, 134

Hunt, Henry, 134

Hunt, Thomas, 134, 147

Huron, Lake, 10, 21, 23, 24, 25, 26, 57, 61, 138

Huron Indians, 9, 10, 57, 99

Hutchins, Thomas, 97

ice ages, 7, 22

Illinois, 7, 13, 53, 65, 71, 77, 80, 83, 102, 117, 119; early explorers in, 55, 56, 57, 59; Native Americans in, 36, 55, 68-69, 126, 129; settlement of, 68, 69; as territory, 51, 68, 90, 103. See also Chicago

Illinois Country, 55, 79, 80

Illinois Indians, 57, 116

Illinois River, 56, 57, 59

Illinois Territory, 50, 68, 90, 103

Indiana, 7, 15, 33, 47, 71, 77, 88, 102; early explorers in, 78; Native Americans in, 36, 55, 78, 89, 90-91; settlement of, 14, 89, 90, 91; as territory, 68, 89-90, 91, 123

About the Author

Kieran Doherty is a longtime journalist and business writer as well as a nonfiction writer for young adults. In addition to writing *Voyageurs, Lumberjacks, and Farmers: Pioneers of the Midwest,* he is the author of four other books in the **Shaping America** series: *Explorers, Missionaries, and Trappers: Trailblazers of the West; Puritans, Pilgrims, and Merchants: Founders of the Northeastern Colonies; Ranchers, Homesteaders, and Traders: Frontiersmen of the South-Central States;* and *Soldiers, Cavaliers, and Planters: Settlers of the Southeastern Colonies.* An avid sailor, he lives in Lake North, Florida, with his wife, Lynne.

Photo Credits